THE MOTHER
OF THE
LITTLE FLOWER

*"Who shall find a valiant woman?
Far and from the uttermost coasts is the
price of her. The heart of her husband
trusteth in her, and he shall have no need
of spoils . . . Her children rose up, and
called her blessed . . ."*

Proverbs 31:10, 28-30

MADAME MARTIN AT THE AGE OF 35.

THE MOTHER
OF THE
LITTLE FLOWER

ZÉLIE MARTIN
1831–1877

By
Celine Martin
(Sister Geneviève of the Holy Face)

Translated from the French by
Fr. Michael Collins, S.M.A.

THE SISTER OF ST. THÉRÈSE
TELLS US ABOUT HER MOTHER

TAN Books
Charlotte, North Carolina

Nihil Obstat: Edward Gallen
                   Censor Deputatus

Imprimi Potest: ✠ John Charles [McQuaid]
                   Archbishop of Dublin
                   Primate of Ireland
                   Dublin, November 21, 1957

First published in December, 1957, by M. H. Gill and Son, Ltd., Dublin. Reprinted in 2005 by TAN Books by permission of the Office Central de Lisieux.

ISBN: 978-0-89555-811-4

Anyone who has received favors through the intercession of Louis and/or Zélie Martin may make them known to the Carmel of Lisieux, 37 rue du Carmel, 14100 Lisieux, France, or to the Postulator General of the Discalced Carmelites, Corso d'Italia 38, 00198 Roma, Italy.

Printed and bound in the United States of America.

TAN Books
Charlotte, North Carolina
www.TANBooks.com
2015

"Our mother was abnegation personified, gifted with great courage, and an extraordinarily energetic character. She had a very sensitive and very generous heart, turned always to God, in whom she had a truly heroic confidence."

—*The sisters of St. Thérèse*

Letter of His Excellency Msgr. Picaud, Bishop of Bayeux and Lisieux, to Sister Geneviève of the Holy Face, of the Carmel of Lisieux.

Bayeux, May 3, 1954.

My dear Daughter in Jesus Christ,

Your Mother Prioress has asked you to take up your pen again in order to give us, as a diptych, together with that of your "admirable father," the portrait of your "incomparable mother."

Wholeheartedly, I give my blessing to this undertaking which completes the work that I had suggested to you and your sisters, ever since my arrival in the Diocese of Bayeux. I have always been convinced that you alone were the qualified witnesses to give the moral characteristics of your parents, who may be considered as providential models, to be held up for the imitation of our modern fathers and mothers of families. The tasks and obligations imposed on the latter are so heavy and laborious that it is right to encourage them by holding up the shining light of such examples. We have no right to keep them hidden.

Doubtless, Mme. Martin's most lively and entertaining correspondence has already made known many aspects of her virtue. It has won for her many sympathetic admirers, but does not her humility hide away several other noble characteristics? Your personal remembrances, in addition to those of your older sisters, will succeed in revealing her completely to us.

I offer you, therefore, my dear Daughter, my most paternal good wishes for a widespread distribution of your filial testimony regarding your father and mother. It will give glory to God, and, at the same time, to your saintly sister, the blessed fruit of grace of that chaste union.

✠ François-Marie
Bishop of Bayeux and Lisieux.

NOTICE

The moral portrait of the father of St. Thérèse of the Child Jesus, outlined by our dear Sister Geneviève of the Holy Face, has aroused in many readers and friends the desire of having similar testimony in regard to the mother of our saint.

We ourselves feel very strongly how appropriate and right it is to collect all these precious memories of the last surviving member of that blessed family, and we heartily agree with so legitimate a desire. None of these treasures should be lost, for their good to souls becomes more and more striking. We are aware especially of a growing movement, the echoes of which reach us from all parts of the world, of veneration for and confidence in the saintly parents of St. Thérèse of the Child Jesus.

That explains the object of this booklet, in which Sister Geneviève of the Holy Face completes with her pen the description of her heroic mother, whom her artistic talent had already helped us to know and to love.

The Carmelites of Lisieux.

PREFACE

I was only eight years and four months old when my mother died. Consequently, my recollections of her are necessarily limited. But at the time of the publication of *The Story of a Soul* and of *The Story of a Family*, I very often questioned my older sisters about our mother. In that way I collected many notes which concern her.

It is this collection of notes and facts assembled by Mother Agnes of Jesus and myself, that constituted the basic documentation for *The Story of a Family*. On that account, also, *The Story of a Family* may be considered as having been completely inspired by us. It is authentic.

In this particular collection, dealing especially with my mother, for the sake of greater clearness, I shall place under different headings my own recollections and those from our family archives. The restricted scope of this booklet does not permit the publication of her many letters (about two hundred letters have been printed).[1] But I shall give extracts from them which will reveal, better than any other interpretation, her richly gifted personality. Besides, I intend borrowing widely from the letters of her older sister, a Visitation nun in Mans, who was her intimate confidante. I shall also

---

[1]. In the Annals of St. Thérèse of Lisieux. Later on they will be published in a special edition.

quote from the letters of my own sister, Marie, who lived at home the last two years of my mother's life.

When in the course of my recollections I use the term "saint" in regard to my mother, or quote other testimonies which employ the term, I do not intend to give to that expression other than a purely personal and private significance.

And first of all, as a heading for all these testimonies, I place as a façade description the characteristic trait of our mother which was stressed by my sisters at the Process of Beatification and of Canonization of the Servant of God, St. Thérèse of the Child Jesus. This is their testimony:

> *Our mother was abnegation personified, gifted with great courage, and an extraordinarily energetic character. She had a very sensitive and very generous heart, turned always to God, in whom she had a truly heroic confidence.*

> Sister Geneviève of the Holy Face
> and of St. Teresa,
> O.C.D., Carmel of Lisieux
> January 2, 1954.

CONTENTS

APPENDICES

SOME TOPOGRAPHICAL DETAILS OF
ALENÇON

THE MOTHER
OF THE
LITTLE FLOWER

"The good God gave me a father and mother more worthy of Heaven than of earth."

—St. Thérèse of the Child Jesus
Letter 261

MORAL PORTRAIT OF MY MOTHER

Youth

Zélie Guérin, my mother, was born on December 23, 1831, near Alençon, in the township of Gaudelain, where her father, a veteran of the Imperial Army, was enrolled in the constabulary. She was baptized the following day in the local church, and received the name of Marie Azelia. However, she was always known as Zélie.

Her mother, a woman of strong faith, but rather too austere, did not understand her and treated her highly-sensitive nature too harshly, which caused her to write, later on, that her youth was "as sad as a winding-sheet." A single detail shows us the picture: though she would have given anything for it when she was a child, Zélie never had a doll, even the smallest one. She suffered from frequent headaches, and this added to the painful atmosphere.

Together with her older sister, who was to become a Visitation nun, as Sister Marie-Dosithée, Zélie became a day pupil at the boarding school of the Perpetual Adoration, at Alençon, directed by the Sisters of the Sacred Hearts of Picpus. She was a very gifted pupil, and developed a tender and solid piety in that religious atmosphere. A little brother, Isidore, ten years younger, was then in his infancy.

Like her sister, she also wanted, first of all, to dedicate her life to God, and with that in mind she went to the Sisters of St. Vincent de Paul, at the General Hospital of Alençon. But the Sister Superior dissuaded her from the step, perhaps on account of her health. It was in those circumstances that she made the following prayer:

> *My God, since I am not worthy to be Your Spouse like my sister, I shall enter the married state to accomplish Your holy will. I beg You then, let me have many children, and may they all be consecrated to You, my God.*

Having begged the Blessed Virgin Mary to show her how she could provide financially for her future, it happened that on December 8, 1851, in the midst of an absorbing occupation, she distinctly heard, as it were, an interior voice saying to her: *Undertake the making of Point d'Alençon lace.* She, therefore, went to a professional school, but before she had completed the course, she left, to escape the inconsiderate attentions of the director of the establishment.

Towards the close of 1853, she began on her own account the establishment of a centre for making this costly lace.

As my older sisters have stressed, mother was as shrewd in business as she was quick and intelligent. Her energy was extraordinary, and she rapidly became successful in her undertakings.

An influential lady of the world, who admired the beauty and talents of mother, wanted to take her to Paris, perhaps with the intention of having her married advantageously; she categorically refused the proposal. She used to tell of the incident smilingly; the world had absolutely no attraction for her. Heaven soon intervened to trace out her path for her.

One day, as she was crossing St. Leonard's bridge at Alençon, the same inspiration which had directed her in regard to her professional work, now made her feel within herself, on meeting a young man who passed by her on the way: *That is he whom I have prepared for you.*

The two families were unknown to each other; but my grandmother Martin had noticed the outstanding qualities of Zélie Guérin at the lace-making school. She desired to have her as her daughter-in-law, and her maternal insight foresaw in Zélie a real treasure.

On July 13, 1858, Zélie was married to Louis Martin, son of a retired army captain. They went to live in his house, at rue Pont Neuf, in Alençon, where father had opened a watchmaking and jewelry store. He was then 36 years old, while she was to be 27 towards the end of the year.

Family Life

In her letters mother has stated that before marriage she was ignorant of the mysteries of life, and that when she learned them she was troubled, even to tears. Father profited by this circumstance to propose to her his own project of their living together as brother and sister. She agreed to this, in spite of her former desire to have children.

But God had other plans for them. These are clearly indicated in the following dedication of a book on the life of the ninth child, the last and brightest gem of their crown:

> *To the sacred and immortal memory of Louis Joseph Stanislaus Martin and of Marie Zélie Guérin, blessed Parents of St. Thérèse, as an example to all Christian Parents.*[1]

And still more recently, at the occasion of the Canonization of St. Thérèse, we have this other testimony:

> More than ever before, our modern society needed to have recalled to mind, by a *living* example which would magnificently *illustrate* before all eyes, the *sanctity* of the married state, and the observance of the law of conjugal morality.
>
> Who does not see that the providential effect of this canonization goes far beyond the Saint herself? In raising to the Altars the ninth child of Louis Martin and Zélie Guérin, the Church crowns, in the glory of the daughter, the exalted virtues of the two parents who were *the life-spring of a numerous and saintly family, and distinguished models of Christian spouses.*[2]

As a matter of fact, many months later, upon the counsel of their confessor, they both agreed in desiring to have many children in order to offer them to God. They then restored to his family a little boy whom they had temporarily taken into their home, after their vir-

---

1. First Portuguese edition of the *Story of a Soul.*
2. *The Nuptial Liturgy* (Rev. Fr. Croegaert).

ginal agreement, which had been based on a complete union of opinions, of Christian faith and of piety.

It is right, then, that our saintly Thérèse, when writing the story of her life, should render thanks to the Lord, *who allowed her to see the light in a holy soil fragrant with the odor of purity.*

* * *

Always faithful to principle, mother was not afraid of having children. When a woman in the neighborhood had triplets, mother exclaimed: "Oh! happy mother! If I had only twins! But I shall never know that happiness! I am madly fond of children. It is such sweet work to take care of babies."

Her correspondence is filled with these exclamations of maternal joy. After the birth of her little Hélène— who was to die young—she wrote to her brother M. Guérin, April 23, 1865:

> Two weeks ago I went to see the baby, who is boarding out with the nurse. I cannot remember that I ever before felt such a thrill of happiness as when I clasped her in my arms; she smiled so sweetly at me, that I thought I was looking at an angel. Really, it is beyond human words. I don't believe that there was ever before such a charming little girl, or ever will be. O! my sweet Hélène! When shall I have the happiness of possessing you completely? I cannot imagine that I have the privilege of being the mother of such a delightful creature.

Far from taking account of trouble or fatigue, her supernatural confidence made her declare later to her sister-in-law, Madame Guérin, who was in poor health, and was expecting a baby:

> The good Lord fits the back for the burden, and never asks more than we can bear. Very often I have seen my husband worried about my health, while I could not have been calmer. I used to say to him: "Don't be afraid; the good God is with us!" I had, though, loads of work and preoccupations, but I felt that firm confidence of being always helped from Heaven.[3]

Still she admits in another confidential note to her Lisieux family, writing to her sister-in-law:

> If you are to have as many children as I, that will demand a lot of abnegation, and the desire to give many elect souls to Heaven.[4]

At each new birth, she used to make the following prayer:

> Lord, grant me the grace that this child may be consecrated to You, and that nothing may tarnish the purity of its soul. If ever it would be lost, I prefer that You should take it without delay.

Her union with God and the fervor of her prayers, during her months of pregnancy, were so great that she was astonished not to see these pious dispositions mani-

---

3. Letter of May 5, 1871.
4. Letter of February 8, 1870.

festing themselves in her children from the dawn of their intelligence. Before her oldest child, Marie, was four, and her Pauline was not two years old, she expressed her disappointment to her Visitation sister at their apparent lack of piety. The latter wrote this to their brother, Isidore:

> Zélie is already distressed that her children show no signs of piety.[5]

As soon as it was born, the babe had to be baptized without delay. She always made inquiries about the Baptism of her neighbors' children. For hers, it was the very day of their birth—the next morning, if they were born at night—that the Sacrament was to be conferred.

At the birth of Thérèse they had to wait two days before she received the sacramental grace. Mother Agnes, when questioned at the Beatification Process about the reason for this delay, replied:

> It was because they were waiting for the arrival of the godfather. Meanwhile our pious mother was in continual mortal terror. Fearing that some misfortune might happen to the child, she constantly imagined that the little one was in danger.

Mother had nine children, of whom four died in infancy. In agreement with my father she wanted to give to each one the name of "Marie," added to another—that of "Joseph" for the two little boys.

On the 8th of December, 1860, she had asked the Immaculate Virgin to send her a second child, and it

5. Letter of February 2, 1864.

was nine months afterwards that Pauline was born, to be a companion to her sister Marie.

Later on, it was to Pauline that she wrote describing what love she and our father had for their children:

> We lived only for them; they were all our happiness and outside of them we desired no other. For their sakes, nothing gave us trouble; the world meant nothing without them. For myself they compensated for everything. And so I desired to have many of them in order to present them to Heaven.

I said that there was perfect understanding between our parents, even if at first their views might differ on some particular point. Mamma had as much admiration for father as she had affection for him; she allowed him to exercise an authority which was really patriarchal. My sisters have affirmed many times that their union was never clouded by any misunderstanding; my mother's correspondence is filled with this testimony.

It is obvious that she could not live without him even for a few days. The letters which she writes to him generally conclude with such phrases as this one—the true expression of her feelings: "Your wife who loves you more than her own life."

Canon Dumaine, Vicar General of Seez, who baptized Thérèse when he was Assistant at Notre Dame, in Alençon, and knew our family well, gives this testimony:

> In their family life, the union was remarkable, both between the husband and wife, and between the parents and the children.

The Education of Her Children

Mother took an active part in our education. I recollect how she always made us say our morning and evening prayers, and taught us the following formula for the offering of the day:

> My God, I give You my heart; please accept it that no creature, but You alone, my good Jesus, may possess it.

She accustomed us to obey through love, to please the dear Jesus, to make small sacrifices for Him. We had a kind of "rosary" to count these acts ("a rosary of acts"); it was composed of movable beads which one could slide on a string.

This detailed work of child formation was begun early. She wrote to her brother who was anxious about the restlessness of his oldest girl:

> Do not be uneasy if you find your little Jeanne manifesting a temper. That will not prevent her from growing up to be an excellent child later on, and even to be your consolation. I remember how Pauline, up to the age of two, was the same, and how distressed I was about her—and now she is my best. But I must tell you that I did not spoil her, either. Little as she was, I let her get away with nothing— without, however, making a little martyr of her, but she had to give in.[6]

On the same subject we find a letter of Sister Marie-

6. Letter of February 3, 1869.

Dosithée's to her brother, Isidore:

> Zélie wrote me the other day about her little
> girls. She asked Marie if she had not committed a
> certain fault. Marie reflected for a moment to
> examine her conscience and replied: "No, Mamma,
> I did do it" She was then sent to bed, happy, with
> the assurance that "our Lord was in her heart"—her
> small face beaming with joy.
>
> As for little Pauline, when her sisters want to take
> her things, her mother tells her: "Give it away, my
> little girl, and you'll have another pearl in your
> crown!" Pauline then gives in immediately.[7]

Mamma carefully watched over us, and kept away
from us even the shadow of evil. Some time after the
birth of Thérèse, all the girls played at dressing up for
her Baptism in the garden. The housemaid, Louise, got
the idea of making me be a godfather and dressing me
up as a little boy. I was then about four years old. The
procession was under way when mother arrived and
put a stop to the play-acting, while scolding Louise for
the "masculine" exhibition.

She was very exacting with regard to perfect mod-
esty, and our dresses always reached below the knees.

One day, a girl older than any of us came to share in
our games. Mother noticed her undue familiarities and
her mysterious whisperings. She called me, and in the
presence of the other girl, warned me against such
secretive and out of place manners. To remove all dan-

---

7. Letter of January 6, 1866.

ger or suspicion she sent the girl home. Let me add this detail: this girl profited by the lesson, and later entered a religious community.

Mother used to take me on her knees to help me to prepare for Confession. She always aimed at winning confidence in her children. As she was very sympathetic and persuasive, it was difficult to hide anything from her. It was also in that way she helped Marie to become less independent and self-assertive.

Marie has told how, though very young, when she was going to a school, conducted by Sisters, she saw a little girl acting in an unbecoming way. She was indignant and told the incident to Mamma immediately. The latter praised her for her straightforwardness, and encouraged her to have the same candor with regard to herself, in Confession. At the same time, mother put her on her guard, withdrew Marie from that school, and placed her with Pauline as permanent boarders with the Visitation Nuns at Mans.

Her quiet firmness was allied with a gentle understanding. Let me quote an example in my own case, which is found in her correspondence with Pauline.

> Little Céline is a darling. She makes many little sacrifices to obtain her aunt's cure. But sometimes she fails to keep them up. Yesterday evening, in spite of being asked, she refused to give up something to her little sister—I forget what it was. Marie was cross with her and told her she only made the sacrifices that she liked to make, and in that case, it would be much better if she made none at all. I told

Marie that she was not right to discourage her like
that, that so young a child could not be expected to
become a saint all at once, and that one must over-
look some little things.[8]

In her Autobiography, Thérèse referred to the manner in which Mamma formed her character, She did
not allow even those childish gestures or poutings that
amuse grown-up people in children. A look of disap-
proval was sufficient to correct her.

Here is an instance related by my mother in a letter
to Pauline, which refers to Thérèse:

>One morning, before going downstairs I wanted
to kiss Thérèse, but she seemed to be fast asleep, and
I did not like to awaken her. Marie, seeing my hes-
itation, said: "I am sure she is only pretending." So I
bent down towards her to give her a kiss, but she
immediately hid herself under the clothes, saying
with the tone of a spoilt child: "I don't want anyone
to look at me." I was not pleased with her, and told
her so.

>Two minutes afterwards I heard her crying, and to
my great surprise, I noticed her soon after, at my
side. She had managed to get out of her cot
unaided, and in her long nightdress had come
downstairs barefooted. Her face was wet with tears.
"Mamma," she said, throwing herself on my knees,
"I was naughty. Forgive me!" Pardon was quickly
granted. I pressed the little angel to my heart, cov-
ering her with kisses.

8. Letter of November 8, 1876.

When she saw herself so well caressed, she said to me: "Oh, Mamma, how I wish you would wrap me up as when I was a baby. And I'll take my chocolate here at the table." I took the trouble to get her blanket, then I wrapped it around her, as when she was small. It was just as if I were playing with a doll.[9]

That episode reveals her pedagogical method, wherein severity was enveloped in tenderness.

I recall another story which concerns me, and which Mamma also wrote to Pauline at Mans, to keep her in touch with all the home news about her sisters:

Celine is learning to read well, but she is as cute as a fox. After all, she is only four, and, thank God, she gives in easily enough. I must tell you an amusing story about her. Yesterday evening she said to me: "Mamma, I don't like poor people!" I told her that Jesus was not pleased at that, and that He would not love her on that account.

She reasoned on: "I love Jesus very much but I don't want to love the poor, never, never. If I do not love the poor, what does that matter to Jesus? He is, of course, Master, but am I not mistress?"

You could not imagine how animated she was; there was no use reasoning with her. But there is a reason for her dislike for the poor.

Some days ago, she was standing in front of the door with a little friend. A poor girl, who was passing by, stood looking at them with an impudent, mocking air. That did not please Céline, who said to

the girl: "Get away, you, from here." The girl was so
furious that before going off she gave her such a slap
on the cheek that it remained red for a whole hour.

I was encouraging her to pardon the poor child,
but she could not forget the incident and
announced to me yesterday: "You want me to like
the poor that come to give me slaps, and make my
face all red. No, no. I can't love them."

But night brings better ideas. The first word she
said to me this morning was to announce that "she
had made up a fine bouquet of flowers, and that it
was for the Blessed Virgin and for the good Jesus."
Then she added: "Now I love the poor all right."[10]

It was gradually and methodically that she taught us
to overcome ourselves.

* * *

But it was especially with Léonie that Mamma had
the greatest difficulty. She could not win her confidence. There was a kind of mystery in her stubbornness
and her apprehensions, with alternating bursts of affection. Mother prayed a great deal for this child whom
she often saw ill, pouting, and slow of understanding.

She tried, on two different occasions, to place her as
a boarder at the Visitation School of Mans, with her two
sisters, Marie and Pauline; but the nuns could not keep
her. On one of those occasions, Sister M. Dosithée
wrote to her brother and sister-in-law:

10. Letter of July 9, 1873.

I am expecting Zélie tomorrow. It will not be a happy visit, I assure you; she will have to take Léonie home with her. How I pity her, poor, dear sister.[11]

A few days later, she added in another letter (April 10):

I saw Zélie. She was quite resigned. She realizes that when children are not completely normal the parents must be the ones to have the anxiety about them.

With her good judgment, the mother wrote to Pauline:

I never like to beg for exceptions or not to follow the usual regulations. A person is happier, even here below, in carrying out his or her duty with courage.[12]

On the 1st of June of this same year, 1874, mother wrote to her sister-in-law:

I no longer depend on anything but a miracle to change her nature. It is true that I do not deserve a miracle, and yet I hope against all hope. The more complicated she seems to me, the more I am persuaded that the goodness of God will not permit her to remain that way.

When our dear Visitation aunt died, mother confided Léonie very particularly to her heavenly protection. It was soon after that she discovered the key to the whole

---

11. Letter of April 6, 1874.
12. Letters of November-December 1875.

enigma. It was the housemaid who dominated Léonie, more through stupidity than malice, terrorized her secretly, and prevented her from opening up her heart. Mamma quickly put things in order by entirely withdrawing Léonie from such a baneful influence. She then endeavored to win her confidence. When she felt that she had not long to live, all her anxieties were centered on this child. We find in her correspondence passages that manifest her anguish. Thus she admits to our aunt Guérin:

> It is Léonie's future which worries me most. I ask myself: "What will become of her when I am gone?" It frightens me! If the sacrifice of my life were necessary to make a saint of her, I would gladly offer it.[13]

That wish of their becoming saints is constantly expressed for all her children. We read in a letter for All Saints' Day, addressed to her two older girls at the Visitation of Mans:

> You must serve the good God faithfully, my dear girls, and beg to be, one day, in the number of those saints whose feast we celebrate today.[14]

Later on, in October, 1875, she wrote to Pauline:

> You will tell your aunt that I am quite pleased with you, because you are a good girl, very affectionate, very submissive, but not yet pious enough.

---

13. Letter of January 18, 1877.
14. Letter of November 1, 1873.

The following year, she said to her:

> Continue to be a good and holy little girl; and if
> you have not yet the latter quality, make efforts to
> acquire it.

A month afterwards, in referring to her sister Marie,
she said:

> I hope that she will be a good girl, but particu-
> larly I want her to become a saint—and you, too,
> Pauline.

The dear Visitation sister had written that Pauline
would be pious. "Oh!" exclaimed Mamma, "how happy
that has made me!"

Then, apropos of her pilgrimage to Lourdes, she
returned to the idea of Léonie:

> At least, if the Blessed Virgin does not cure me, I
> shall implore her to cure my child, to open up her
> intelligence, and to make a saint of her.[15]

After her return, when her general health had
become worse, as I shall explain later on, she still hoped
for her cure, in order to complete the education of her
children. Hence we have the imploring act of faith
which she sent to Pauline:

> Well, as for myself, I am still hoping for the mir-
> acle from the Goodness and the Almighty Power of
> God, through the intercession of His Blessed
> Mother. Not that I ask Him to remove my ailment

---

15. Letter to her brother, June 11, 1877.

completely from me, but just let me live on for a few years—to have time to educate my children, and especially this dear Léonie, who needs me so much, and who arouses all my pity.

She is less privileged than you in natural gifts, but in spite of that, she possesses a heart desirous of loving and being loved. It is only a mother who can continually show her the love that she needs, and can follow her closely enough to do her constant good.[16]

Mother applied herself with so much persevering diligence that the dear child became entirely and blindly attached to her—even to the point of embarrassment. However, when small sacrifices were required of her, she was not so well pleased. To get her to overcome herself gradually, mother appealed to her gently and lovingly, using different means of encouragement. One way was to have Léonie put a nut into a certain drawer for each act of self-denial. Then mother would go anxiously every evening to look into the drawer—often only to be disappointed.

But Léonie was extremely good at heart. Already in 1875, my mother wrote to her sister-in-law:

I am not dissatisfied with Léonie. If we could overcome her stubbornness, and make her will more flexible, she would become a good, devout girl who would be afraid of nothing. She has a will of iron; when she wants something she triumphs over every obstacle to attain her object.

16. Letter of June 25, 1877.

Let me add that she had good judgment, and to her humility she joined a natural gentleness. But especially she had a "heart of gold," to which mother frequently referred in her letters. Among other points, I mention the following: she used to give up going to Lisieux in order to let me go in her place; and once when she was obliged to go and leave Thérèse and me at home, she said to Thérèse: "Ah, my dear little sister, I'll bring you back all the cakes that will be given to me!"

I return to the quotation of Mother's letter:

> This afternoon I had her beside me in order to get her to recite some prayers; but she was soon tired of that, and begged me: "Mamma, tell me the life of Our Lord!" I had not planned to relate anything; it tires me—my throat is always sore. At last, I made an effort, and I told her the story of Our Lord's life. When I came to the Passion, she began to shed tears. It pleased me to see how she entered into the spirit of it.[17]

The future was to crown the hopes and the invincible confidence of our mother. It was also to justify the prediction of our Visitation aunt, who had foretold that this child, who had occasioned so many tears, would be a saint.

As a matter of fact, after the death of our mother, Léonie corrected herself completely; she lived more than 40 in a monastery, where she edified all by her

---

17. Letter of September 7.

virtues, and where she died a saintly death.[18]

Some have even regarded this successful transformation as the masterpiece of a mother as an educationalist, particularly in such a complicated nature, and one less gifted than those of her sisters.

* * *

Though Mother corrected us for the least sign of defects, she also liked to see us cheerful and full of life. She even willingly played with us, at the risk of having her own day's work prolonged to midnight or after.

Though very simple in her own dress, Mamma enjoyed taking great pains about the dress of her children. Her correspondence gives us glimpses of her natural good taste and simple dignity. Our sister Marie relates a typical instance:

> I was about seven years old at the time. One day we were to wear for the first time our dark blue wool-satin dresses; my mother wanted to see the four of us before we went for a walk. She looked us over for several minutes with a tender, motherly glance of contentment. Then she said simply: "Run along now, my little girls." But she carefully avoided any complimentary remarks about our appearance or the dresses, which I thought so pretty, in order not to arouse any vanity in us.

---

18. At the Visitation Convent of Caen.

Mamma was also very careful to keep us away from temptations to envy at the sight of rich persons. Much later on, she pointed out to Pauline a certain inclination of her older sister to expose herself to that temptation. It was about a walk, in January 1876:

> Marie kept looking at little girls about the same age as Celine and Thérèse. She envied their dresses, and begged me to have her little sisters dressed like them. Some persons are never happy! As a matter of fact, our two younger ones are dressed better than you ever were, but that is not enough when there are still nicer dresses! In spite of that, I have no desire to imitate the rich; it is a real servitude—one becomes a slave of fashion! And yet, you know, Pauline, your sister detests showing off with fancy dresses.

Mother was not narrow-minded and followed the rules of good taste. She candidly confessed: "For myself, I dislike all elaborate dressing up." (November 12, 1876). At the same time she admits to Pauline that she "is careful to have the children well dressed, although always simply." (November, 1875).

When Marie left the convent boarding school, mother did not wish to have her drawn into social affairs, and she refused to let her take part in home dancing parties. After having told her sister-in-law about her decision, she explains it to Pauline:

> I know that Marie has nothing to fear in these young girls' parties; but I do not like to see her

mingling with such rich persons—it arouses
unwholesome ideas of envy. Personally, I never like
to associate with people like that.[19]

A few months before that, she wrote in the same
vein:

We are all inclined more or less to desire what we
do not possess, and when we obtain it we have no
further interest in it.[20]

When writing to Pauline, she jokingly refers to the
same tendency that she notices in Marie:

Here we have Marie who is dreaming of dwelling
in a beautiful house, in Half-moon Street, opposite
the Poor Clares. She talked only of that all yesterday
afternoon. One would think that it was Heaven!
Although your sister is by no means worldly, she is
never happy where she is. She is always seeking
something better; she wants to have beautiful
rooms, large, and well-furnished.

Last Thursday, the nurse's daughter [21] came to visit
us. Marie was delighted and astonished when the
little one stood spellbound at the door of her room,
exclaiming; "Ah! how beautiful it is!" The poor little creature believes there is nothing grander, but
Marie knows better, from her friends of schooldays,
and she dreams of something still finer. If she had
something else she would still feel, perhaps, a need
for something even better. As for me, I think that if

---

19. November 8, 1876.

20. Letter of May 21, 1876.

21. Rose Taille—known as "Little Rose," the nurse of Thérèse.

I owned a magnificent castle, surrounded by everything one could want on earth, I should feel a
greater lack than if I were alone in a small attic cell,
forgetting the world, and being forgotten by it.[22]

* * *

Being an excellent housekeeper, Mother trained
Marie so well in her household duties, that the latter
was perfectly capable of taking her place in that respect,
when mother was taken from us.

Although she could not bear wasting things, she
spared nothing when there was question of our education and spiritual welfare.

Money is nothing when there is question of one's
sanctification or the perfection of a soul.[23]

These lines were written at the time of a retreat made
by Marie at the Visitation Convent of Mans. The spiritual fruit of her maternal education was maturing, since
she could write:

Marie has ideas that please me; worldly ideas do
not penetrate her mind as much now as spiritual
ones. Yet she has a long way to go before fully
entering on the way to perfection. However, she is
strongly inclined that way already.[24]

The mother could also write about Léonie:

---

22. Letter of January 16, 1876.
23. Letter to Pauline, May 10, 1877.
24. Letter to Pauline, May 14, 1876.

She hears so much talk about the next life, that she often refers to it, herself, also.[25]

* * *

The different quotations which I have given from Mother's letters show both their charm and their educational influence. Marie often told us of those she had received to help her to prepare for her First Communion which was made, contrary to the usual custom, when she was nine. Unfortunately, all these were destroyed by the maid, who thoughtlessly burned them. Marie, who always brought them home with her at vacation time, in order to keep them securely, was heartbroken to have been deprived of them!

The letters, many times more numerous, which were sent to Pauline, who stayed on alone for two years at the school, have been preserved. These letters were the delight not only of the recipient, but also of her teachers, who declared to her: "No other pupil receives letters like these from her parents." And the nuns passed them around among the members of the community.

It would be impossible to express how tenderly and respectfully we all loved our parents. At home, I never heard any one of us say a disrespectful word to them, or even something a little too familiar. None of us, except Léonie before her transformation, would ever argue

---

25. Letter to Pauline, May 14, 1876

about an order given by them. It never crossed our minds; we obeyed so completely through love.

In their prayers for their parents, Marie and Pauline used to change "papa and mamma" into "mamma and papa" by turn, in order not to show any priority to one over the other!

Both of them declared, in the Beatification Process for Thérèse:

> We were never spoiled. Mother watched very carefully over the souls of her children; even the slightest fault was pointed out to be corrected. It was a kind and loving education, but always vigilant and careful.

Mother had a kind of predilection for Pauline, but we were all so well beloved that none of us felt jealous of any preference. It was mother, through her charming stories, who sowed in Pauline's soul the desire for virginity. Mother Agnes of Jesus was to testify at the Process of Beatification:

> My parents always seemed to me to be saints. We were filled with respect and admiration for them. I sometimes asked myself if it were possible to find their equals on earth. Around me I could see nothing like them.

The nuns of the Visitation held the same opinion. They assured my older sisters: "None of their boarding companions could glory in having a mother like theirs; such a one did not exist."

As for me, it was especially my venerable father whom I knew better; but I always keep a touching recollection of that incomparable mother.

Life of Labor

There are many witnesses to testify that Mother was activity personified. She was constantly busy with her lace-making, housekeeping, working for her children, and her correspondence. Father endeavored as far as he could to relieve her, persuading her to accept helpers. But she never thought of herself—she forgot herself entirely.

Her former housemaid, Louise, wrote to the Carmel many long years afterwards:

> How many details have come to my mind since
> her death! For herself, anything was good enough,
> but for others, it was quite the reverse![26]

I myself can still remember her distinctly, preparing every morning an excellent breakfast for all in the house; whereas she was satisfied to snatch a little soup for herself which she swallowed hastily, as she was going about.

Always the last to retire, around 11 p.m., she often rose at 5:30 a.m. She sometimes referred good-humoredly to her "wretched" Point d'Alençon, which was a constant worry to her. On the one hand, she did not wish to leave her workers idle; on the other, it was by this assiduous occupation that she aimed at

26. Mme. Le Gendre, July 22, 1923.

securing dowries for her children.

She explains her position to Mme. Guérin;

> I have another worry that troubles me: my lace
> business is not going well. I know that will only
> make you laugh; you will say, "So much the better,
> it is time for you to stop." You are quite right; I
> would say the same thing, but there is something
> that prevents me. What is urging me is not to gain
> more money; I have more than I ever desired. But I
> believe it would be folly on my part to abandon this
> enterprise, when I have to provide for my five chil-
> dren; I must work for them to the very end. And
> besides, I am anxious, too, for my working women,
> to whom I cannot give employment, although oth-
> ers get plenty to do. That troubles me more than
> anything else.
>
> My poor Marie feels the whole situation very
> much, also. She has not a good word for the Point
> d'Alençon. She repeats that she would rather live in
> an attic than to earn her living at what it costs me.
> I admit that she is not wrong. If I were free and
> alone, and if I had to go through all I have suffered
> for the past 25 years, I would prefer to starve; the
> very thought of it gives me the "creeps."
>
> I often say that if I endured half of all this in order
> to gain Heaven, I would be a canonizable saint! I
> think of my brother, also; if he has the same worries
> as I, I pity him with all my heart, for I know well
> what is the price per yard.[27]

---

27. Letter of February 6, 1876.

In all these annoyances and disappointments our father carried half the burden. We find this expressed in a letter to Pauline:

> Your father is soon to go to Paris about the Point d'Alençon which isn't going well. He is thinking of taking Marie with him; he imagines that he would get on better if she accompanied him.[28]

On the whole, and more frequently, she complains that the lace-making is going too well; she cannot carry out all the orders which she receives. Hence we find this sigh of regret after a restful trip to Lisieux, where the two older girls had stayed on:

> When Marie and Pauline come back home, there will be no further holidays and joys, and they will find it hard. Even for myself, I found it trying to get back to the harness; the work seemed more tedious than usual.[29]

The following year she confided to Pauline:

> I long for rest. I have not even the courage to struggle on. I feel the need of quiet reflection to think of salvation, which the complications of this world have made me neglect.
>
> And yet I should remind myself of the words of the *Imitation*—"Why do you seek repose, since it is for work that you are born?" But when your work absorbs you and when you no longer have the

---

28. Letter of January 16, 1876.
29. Letter to Mme. Guérin, August 22, 1875.

energy of youth, you cannot help wishing to be free of it, at least somewhat so. Well, it is with that hope that I live on.[30]

However, when Mother was overburdened with care, she had recourse to prayer for a renewal of courage. It was with heartfelt conviction she used to say: "The good God who is a Father never sends His children more than they can bear."

Often she experienced this direct help. Formerly, she had comforted her brother when he was having trials and losses in his business. This proves that in her apparent discouragement she was sustained by a supernatural strength.

Thus, on February 14, 1868, she wrote to her brother:

> You must be courageous and not worry so much. I used to be like you when I started my lace enterprise, to the point of being actually ill about it. Now, I am more sensible. I am much less apprehensive, and am resigned to whatever annoying things happen, or may happen. I repeat that the good Lord permits it all that way, and I don't worry any further.

Sometime later on she was to write:

> It is over little things that I worry most. Whenever a real misfortune happens, I am quite resigned, and I await with confidence the help of God.[31]

---

30. Letter of November 8, 1876.
31. Letter to her sister-in-law, September 29, 1875.

Some months before her death, her optimistic character manifested itself in these lines:

> I have scarcely any reason for being glad that time is marching on, but I am like children who do not worry about the morrow: and I, too, am always looking forward to happiness.[32]

A last word on her own work may be summed up in these words of hers:

> I am happiest at my window putting together my "Point d' Alençon."[33]

With her own personal experience of daily work, the servants were the object of great concern to her; as a result, they remained long in her service. The servants for us were part of the family. It was on that account when it was decided to dismiss the maid who had so wrongly treated Léonie, the poor girl wept so much that she was allowed to stay, to take care of Mamma, whose illness was making frightful progress.

In a letter to Uncle Guérin, my mother summed up her social ideas in regard to the treatment of servants:

> It is not always a question of higher wages which is at the root of the attachment of servants to a family. They must feel that they are loved; we should show them sympathy and not be too exacting towards them. When they have a good background, they will certainly render service with affection and devotedness.

32. December 31, 1876.
33. Letter to Mme. Guérin, September 22, 1872.

You know how quick I am, and yet all the maids
that I have had loved me, and I keep them as long
as I wish. The one I have at present would fall ill if
she were sent away. I am certain that if she were
offered 200 francs more she would not wish to leave
us. But it is true also that I treat my maids just as I
treat my own children.[34]

Her women workers received the same affectionate
care and attention. Sunday afternoons, after Vespers, she
used to visit those who were ill, taking them material
help, together with moral encouragement.

Spirit of Faith and Christian Life

All Mother's correspondence points to the great care
she always took to give God first place, to consider Him
as a Father, and to look on all events from the point of
view of faith.

Referring to excellent friends of hers, who were very
charitable, but who considered God as being too
mighty and distant to take a particular interest in our
little lives, she wrote:

It makes me sad that such good people should
have such thoughts. I believe that the good Lord
takes an active interest in us. I have experienced it
many times in my life, and how many proofs I have
of His watchfulness, which I can never forget![35]

---

34. Letter of March 2, 1868.
35. Letter to Pauline. March 12, 1876.

She was completely detached from all earthly goods, and it was natural for her to look down on the things of this world. Her soul was attached only to the realities of the future life. I can still hear her reciting passages of poetry which she had learned; it was always poetry with a melancholy tone, because for her this life was truly an exile.

In a letter to her brother, we find an echo of her intimate conversations with her Visitation sister: "We spend our time together, speaking of a mysterious, angelic world." [36]

When the sister had gone to her reward Mother wrote to Pauline:

> My spirit is no longer here below; it is off in the celestial spheres, and I am unable to entertain you with any earthly interests. [37]

In the Process of Beatification, Marie testified:

> My father and mother had a deep faith. In listening to them speak of eternity, we were disposed, although quite young at the time, to look on all things of this world as pure vanity.

Mamma used to repeat wholeheartedly:

> True happiness is not to be found in this world. It is a complete loss of time to try to find it here. [38]

---

36. Letter March 5, 1865
37. Letter March 12, 1877.
38. Letter to her sister-in-law, February 12, 1870.

Or again:

> Under what illusions do the majority of men live!
> If they have wealth, they want to have honors also.
> And when they obtain them they are still unhappy,
> for the heart which seeks anything outside of God is
> never satisfied. How true it is that one is never really
> happy in this world! I know people who have
> acquired a great fortune, and who feel insecure and
> unhappy just because of their riches.[39]

Thus, she had no esteem for the goods of this world,
and did not consider those who possessed them any
better on that account. Once when she was referring to
a young woman of whom she had been fond, but who,
after a rich marriage, would no longer recognize her,
she added:

> That incident detaches my heart more and more
> from the world which is false. I do not want to be
> attached to anyone except God and my family.[40]

I could multiply quotations from her letters on that
point. I will limit myself to a few more which express
her thoughts more explicitly. In telling her brother,
when he was a young man, about the tragic death of a
married couple who believed themselves the happiest
creatures in the world, she concludes:

> I always heard it said "Woe, a triple woe, to those
> who make such a statement." Dearest brother, I am

---

39. Letter to her sister-in-law, November 12, 1876.
40. Letter to her brother and sister-in-law, July 21, 1872.

personally so convinced of what I say, that at certain times, when I am feeling happy, I dare not think about it, without a certain apprehension. For it is certain, and proved by experience, that there is no real happiness here below. No! it cannot be found on earth, and it is rather a bad sign when everything prospers. In His wisdom, God has arranged things that way to remind us that this earth is not our true home.[41]

Worn out by her crushing duties, she foresees that she is shortening her days ; she admits it to her brother:

If I did not have children to bring up and educate I should welcome death with joy, as we are gladdened by the quiet, clear dawn of a bright day.[42]

Mother had wanted to enter the religious life, as I have already said; sometimes she felt homesick for it. But she never on that account lost sight of the duties of her state. She wrote resignedly to our uncle:

I often think of my saintly sister and of her quiet, peaceful life. She works, but not to gain perishable riches; she is active only for Heaven, which she is ever looking forward to and longing for. As for me, I see myself bent towards the earth, toiling with all my strength to amass gold which I cannot take with me, and which I have no desire to take. What could I do with it in the next life? Sometimes I almost regret that I did not become a nun like her,

---

41. Letter to her brother, March 28, 1864.
42. Letter of May 3, 1867.

but . . . immediately I say to myself: "But I would not have my four little girls, and my darling Joseph!" No! it is better for me to toil on, as I am, and to have them with me. Provided that I reach Heaven with my dear Louis, and that I see them all there, even better placed than myself, I shall be happy; I do not ask for anything more.[43]

Many years later she wrote to Pauline in the same way:

I dream only of solitude and the cloister. With the ideas I have I really don't know why the religious life was not my vocation, either to remain single or to be enclosed in a convent. Now I should like to live to an advanced old age, in order that, when my children are provided for, I might retire into solitude. But I feel, too, that even those are only empty ideas, and so I scarcely consider them seriously. It is better to employ the present usefully than to be musing about the future.[44]

In the far-off early days of her marriage, these same thoughts had made her shed abundant tears. Writing again to Pauline, and referring to them, she tried to excuse them while revealing her intimate feelings:

In your tender love for your father, you must think that I grieved him by my tears. I don't think so; he understood me and tried to console me, as well as he could, for he had the same tastes as I.

---

43. Letter of May 3, 1867.
44. Letter of January 16, 1876.

I believe that our love for each other was even
increased. We always thought alike; he was always a
source of consolation and of strength to me.[45]

Such was always their attitude towards each other.

Hence we can understand the happiness our mother
felt in talking with her dear Visitation nun about
supernatural subjects, in her parlor visits, or by correspondence—unfortunately destroyed. What happy
moments they were, which renewed her spiritual
strength! It can be easily understood how great a void
the death of her beloved sister left in her heart.

Before it took place she tried to prepare her little
boarder in the Visitation of Mans by giving her the
consoling thoughts with which she herself was upheld.

Have courage, my dear Pauline; whatever the
good Lord sends us, we should submit to it. If I lose
my dear sister I shall not weep for her, but for
myself. She will be happy; it is we who will have
sorrow. But this sorrow will be soothed by the certainty of her happiness.[46]

She stresses this thought when writing to her sister-
in-law:

It is sad indeed; but we shall always have the consolation of knowing that she is in Heaven. For me
that is the one essential point.[47]

---

45. Letter of March 4, 1877.
46. Letter of October 29, 1876.
47. Letter of December 7, 1876.

Mother was very humble. In her letters, she frequently accused herself of her imperfections:

> I often say during the day: "My God, how I wish I were a saint!" But then I do not accomplish the works of a saint.[48]

One All Saints' Day, she insisted with charming simplicity:

> I want to become a saint; it will not be easy at all. I have a lot of wood to chop[49] and it is as hard as stone. I should have started sooner, while it was not so difficult; but, in any case, "better late than never."[50]

She has the same ambition for all those who are dear to her. We find her writing to her brother:

> I am glad to see that people think well of you; you will attain a position of honor. That makes me happy, but above all, I want you to become a saint. However, before desiring sanctity for others, I should do well to take the road to it myself, which I am not doing; but I hope that will come, too.[51]

Despite her poor opinion of herself, however, she led a very mortified life, and was rigorously faithful to the laws of fasting and abstinence (which were then much more strict than they are now). She was perhaps even

---

48. Letter to Pauline, February 26, 1876.
49. i.e., much hard work to accomplish (translator).
50. To Marie and Pauline, November 1, 1873.
51. Letter of March 19, 1874.

too rigorous—or so her Visitation sister thought, and also her children. Sister M. Dosithée wrote to her brother and sister-in-law in regard to Mother:

> None of the family is strong, nor the mother either. She has pains in her back and chest, and has been coughing all winter. She would be a very great loss to her family. I wanted her to consult a physician before undertaking the Lenten fast which she wishes to keep.[52]

Mother observed these penitential exercises strictly, even in her last illness. Some months before her death in December, 1876, she was going to Lisieux to consult a noted surgeon. She writes to her brother to remind him that it is Ember Week, and that she desires to follow the Church's regulations (of fast and abstinence). She forestalls his decision for her when she writes:

> You know that those are fast days; and I fast, as I am not ill enough to feel myself dispensed; so let there be no meal prepared for me.

Her merit was all the greater, inasmuch as she admitted in confidence how much fasting cost her. In a letter to M. Guérin during Lent, we read:

> We are in the full period of penance. Fortunately, it will soon be over, for I suffer so much from fasting and abstinence. It is not, however, such a hard mortification, but I feel my stomach so weak, and

52. Letter of February 8, 1874.

especially I feel so cowardly that if I listened to myself, I would not want to do anything at all.[53]

The following year she wrote to Pauline:

Only 21 days more, but 21 days that pass by slowly, for we must carry out our Lenten regulations. It is so tiring!

. . . I must close my letter, for it is already late, and I rise early. I find that difficult also, with the Lenten fast. How I long for Easter![54]

Nothing could prevent our parents from fulfilling the laws of fast and abstinence, even in the presence of strangers. On the unexpected arrival of a friend, my mother was very pleased that he was invited to stay elsewhere. She writes:

Yesterday evening, I was rather pleased that he was not staying with us, on account of the fast. He would have been obliged to eat his supper alone, and so he would have been ill at ease, and we, also.[55]

Mother lived a life of deep piety. Every morning she assisted with my father at the 5:30 Mass; both of them went to Holy Communion as often as the custom of that time permitted. In addition to that, on Sundays they assisted at the Solemn High Mass, and at Vespers.

For the Sunday Vespers, so often neglected by many

---

53. Letter March 14, 1875. It is to be noted that my mother practiced a strict fast—not taking anything before mid-day; in the evening only a light collation of some ounces.

54. Letter March 26, 1876.

55. Letter to her sister-in-law, March 14, 1875.

Christians, Mother would cut short visits and other occupations, without apology. Her letters frequently testify to her fidelity on this point.

A few Sundays before her death, she still dragged herself to church, leaning on the arm of one of the family.

She would not on any account omit her First Friday Communion. As will be noted later on, she went with father for the last time in August, 1877, although worn out by suffering, and obliged to stop at every step of the way.

Morning and evening prayers were recited in common, as well as grace before and after meals; all the feasts were celebrated in a family spirit.

In this connection, I should like to draw attention particularly to the celebration of the *feast* which occurs each week: *Sunday.* My mother used to praise Father for his strict observance of this holy day, attributing to it the prosperity of the family. She predicted the same to her brother and sister-in-law, who were then suffering from a financial set-back.

> . . . I have firm hope that this time of trial will not last. What gives me a confidence which nothing can diminish is especially the edifying manner with which you sanctify Sunday. All faithful observers of the Lord's Day, perfect or imperfect, are blessed in their enterprises; in the end, in one way or another they become rich.[56]

---

56. Letter September 29, 1873. The prediction was realized, for 16 years later M. and Mme. Guérin received a very rich legacy.

She herself scrupulously adhered to the Sunday observance. Regarding a journey, she wrote, November 26, 1871:

> I shall take the train for Lisieux Sunday morning at 3:30. This time I find it impossible to travel on Saturday, and I cannot travel all Sunday morning. That would be against my principles, for I think we should take great care not to give ourselves to what may be Sunday work.[57]

Later on, when in her serious illness, she had to join the pilgrimage to Lourdes on Sunday, she wrote:

> The good Lord knows well that we could not do otherwise. We shall take the afternoon train, in order to be able to assist at all the morning services.[58]

Mother had regular recourse to the parish priest of Montsort for Confession and direction. She attended all the meetings of the Third Order of St. Francis, of which she was a member, at the Poor Clares' Convent. She visited these nuns, recommending herself to their prayers in her problems and sufferings.

She was also inscribed in the Archconfraternity of the Agonizing Heart of Jesus, as well as in other religious associations.

We must acknowledge, however, that she knew how to choose. She disliked certain practices of devout persons, which by their subtleties and complications are opposed

---

57. Letter to her brother, November 26, 1871.
58. Letter to Pauline, May 1877.

to the Gospel spirit in its strong, virile simplicity.

Mother not only took part in the parish services, over and above the days of obligation—as we find in a letter written two months before her death: "The bell for Benediction is ringing, and I want to go"[59]—but she would not dispense herself from assisting at sermons even during the week.

Often, this called for real heroism! In one of her letters, after having said that "in spite of a fever, which has been weakening me for six weeks," and while carrying a baby, she was doing all her work as usual, she adds: "I have even arisen every morning at 5:30 for the past two weeks to go to St. Leonard's to assist at the Mission, given by the Capuchin Fathers."[60]

On another occasion, she candidly confesses that it is only "for duty's sake" that she goes to hear some sermons.

She greatly enjoyed the ecclesiastical chant, particularly when it was simple. She did not care for church hymns, or for Mass music which seemed elaborate or theatrical.

* * *

Mother had an intense devotion to the Blessed Virgin Mary; she admitted that she had frequently received signal graces through her intercession.

She begged her brother, who was then carrying on

---

59. Letter to her brother, June 7, 1877.
60. Letter to her sister-in-law, February 12, 1870.

his medical studies in Paris, to light votive candles for
her intention, at the Shrine of Our Lady of Victories,
a Marian sanctuary very dear to our family. As she knew
that he was very much exposed to the allurements of
the capital, she gave him the following advice:

> If you only agree to do something I am going to
> ask you, and if you want to offer me that for a New
> Year's gift, I should be happier than if you sent me
> all Paris. Here it is! You live close to Our Lady of
> Victories. Very well! Go in, just once a day to say an
> *Ave Maria* to her. You will see that she will protect
> you in a quite particular way, and that she will make
> you succeed in this world and give you an eternity
> of happiness hereafter. What I am saying to you is
> not just an exaggerated and unfounded pious state-
> ment. I have good reason to trust in Our Lady. I
> have received graces from her of which I alone
> know.[61]

That was why the statue of Our Lady, which was to
smile on Thérèse as a child, was always venerated by her
with honor. One day Marie, our eldest sister, thinking
this statue too big for the room in which it was placed,
said: "It looks like a school statue," and wanted to have
it changed. Mamma protested at once:

> When I am gone, child, you can do what you
> like, but as long as I live, this Blessed Virgin will not
> leave this place.

---

61. Letter of January 1, 1863.

It was at the foot of this statue that she made us say our prayers, and we used to kiss it so often that its fingers were all broken, and it was necessary to keep in reserve more than one pair of hands!

During May we used to assist at the May devotions in the church. Besides that, Mother wanted to keep a special month of Mary at home. The shrine had to be so beautiful that my sister used to joke about it, good-naturedly, and say "that it rivaled the decorations of the parish church," Notre Dame, Alençon.

It is true that it was gorgeous, for besides lace hangings over a blue background, Mamma used to hire a poor woman to bring whole armfuls of flowers and blossoms from the country, and branches of white thorn. These were placed in vases and reached up to the ceiling, to the great delight of little Thérèse who would clap her hands with glee.

Among the extraordinary graces attributed to the protection of this statue—now known as *Our Lady of the Smile*—I must mention this particular one, which I often heard Mother tell.

After the death of little Hélène, at the age of five, my mother recalled a slight untruth which the child had told. She blamed herself for not having brought a priest to confess the dying child, lest she should have to expiate the fault in Purgatory. While she was in prayer before the Madonna, and reviewing her own negligence with a certain anguish, a heavenly voice whispered to her with marvellous sweetness: "She is there beside me" (in Heaven). At this reply of the Divine

Mother, inexpressible joy took the place of her anxiety.

It should be noted, also, that it was the privilege of the Immaculate Conception of the Blessed Virgin Mary that our mother always honored. Each year her feast of December 8th was celebrated with a very heartfelt devotion. On that morning she was the first at church. She lighted a votive candle at the feet of Mary and expressed all her requests and desires with trusting gratitude.

Such was the 8th of December, 1860, to which I have already referred. Requesting the Virgin most pure to grant her a second little girl, she implored her—according to her own expression—"as a little girl begs for a doll from her mother." This living doll was baby Pauline, born the following September 7th. Later on, in relating to Pauline this far-off memory, Mother wrote:

> This year again, I am going to find Our Lady early in the morning. I want to be the first arrival. I shall give her my candle as usual but I shall not ask her for any more little daughters. I shall only pray to her that those she has given me may all become saints, and that I may follow them closely; but they must be much better than I.[62]

Her confidence in the miracles of Our Lady of Lourdes was remarkable. She earnestly joined in spirit the pilgrimages which Father made there, although, personally, traveling had no attraction for her. Thus she confided to her sister-in-law:

---

62. Letter of December 5, 1875.

As for myself, I dislike traveling: there is only one journey for which I should feel any attraction; that would be to go and visit the Holy Land.[63]

Nevertheless, it was to Lourdes that she resorted at the end of her life, hoping to obtain a cure.

She always took a great interest in the historical interventions of the Blessed Virgin. During the darkest days of the war of 1870, it was with great interest that she read, in the Catholic press, about the apparitions of our Blessed Mother to the children of Pontmain.

Her faith, however, was not drawn to the marvellous or extraordinary. At that time there were many rumors and alleged prophecies; but she was rather inclined to joke about them.

* * *

I cannot refer to our mother's devotion for the Queen of Heaven without recalling also the devotion she felt for St. Joseph: one led to the other. It was to this great saint that she attributed the cure of Thérèse when a baby only a few weeks old, as her correspondence points out.

In spite of contrary suggestions or desires, she would have given the name of Joseph to a third baby boy, if that joy had been granted to her. After the birth of Thérèse, she wrote to her brother, not without a touch of humor:

---

63. Letter of September 7, 1875.

Even before the baby was born, Sister M. Dosithée, imagining that it was going to be a boy, had written to me asking me not to give him the name of Joseph but Francis—as if she suspected that good St. Joseph had taken the others away from me! I replied to her that whether the new little boy would die or not, it was Joseph he would be called.[64]

If in my mother's life we may notice graces that are almost tangible, owing to her confident prayers, there can hardly be found any extraordinary phenomena. One cannot consider as such those interior inspirations in regard to her choice of work and to her marriage, to which I have already referred. The favors obtained through her fervent recourse to our Blessed Mother, likewise cannot be classed as extraordinary.

Mamma has, nevertheless, related an incident which happened to her one day, as she was finishing some spiritual reading in which there was question of diabolical vexations. "Such outrages will not happen to me," she sighed with relief. "Only saints have reason to fear those things." At that very moment a terrific grip seized her by the shoulder but immediately a trustful prayer sprang from her lips and she regained her usual serenity.

It must be noted that at that time she was awaiting the birth of her who was to be the little St. Thérèse. Besides, she attached no importance to the incident; she preferred to live her life of pure, simple faith, in childlike security.

---

64. Letter of March 1, 1873.

* * *

It was with this supernatural certainty that the experiences of life were viewed.

Her brother, M. Guérin, in business at Lisieux, met with frequent losses, in the course of his professional life; particularly at first, when he wanted to add a drugstore to his chemist shop. Mother felt as concerned and saddened as if it were a question of her own personal interests. At the same time, she encouraged him with supernatural thoughts, such as the following:

> My sister spoke a great deal to me about your business . . . I told her not to worry so much about all that, and that there was only one thing to do: to pray to Our Lord about it, for neither she, nor I, can help you in any other way. But He, who knows how to manage things, will come to our rescue, when we have suffered enough. Then you will realize that it is neither to your aptitude, nor to your intelligence, that you owe your success, but to God alone. I have had the same experience with my Point d'Alençon. It is a very salutary conviction. I have known it myself.
>
> You know that we are all inclined to pride. I often notice that those who have amassed a large fortune generally are unbearably self-satisfied. I am not suggesting that I, or you, either, should come to that; but we should have both been more or less tainted with pride. Besides, it is certain that constant prosperity draws the heart away from God. And He does not lead His elect by that way; they first pass

through the crucible of suffering, to be purified therein.[65]

After a fire, which caused great distress to the dear Lisieux family, Mamma wrote to her sister-in-law:

> We must exercise much faith and resignation to bear this loss without murmuring, and to accept with submission the holy Will of God.
>
> I know that you place your confidence in the Goodness of God. That convinces me that you will come out of this affliction much better than you think.
>
> Mme. Y. appears to be very much happier than you. She lives only for wealth and pleasure, and gives her mid-Lent parties. However, believe me, I prefer to see you with your losses, than to risk seeing you, like her, forgetting Heaven, for the short-lived pleasures of this life.[66]

Love of the Church—Efficacy of Prayer

Mother had a veritable cult for the Church, for the Pope, and for the priesthood in general. It was a source of grief for her that the Holy Father was exposed to persecution, and that he was virtually a prisoner within the Vatican. On account of her love for the Church, she was completely overcome when the reports published the excesses of the Paris Commune, with the massacre

---

65. Letter to M. Guérin, July 1872.
66. Letter of March 30, 1873.

of the hostages. Her prayers for the welfare of the Church and of France were at that time most fervent.

Never would our mother criticize the clergy. In our home it never occurred to us to refer to the defects of priests.

As I have already said, she followed the Commandments of the Church strictly and went so far as to avoid purchasing anything on Sunday, or making any train journeys. She had a heartfelt devotion to the Church Suffering, and procured the celebration of Masses for the Poor Souls. At her father's death, she arranged for the speedy celebration of 150 Masses, while resolving to have others said a little later on.

At the death of Sister M. Dosithée, she immediately sent an offering to the Visitation in order to have Masses said without delay.

Her love for the Church drew her into a heartfelt interest in the Propagation of the Faith; in agreement with Father she gave, each year, a very generous donation to that work. All manifestations of Catholic faith aroused her enthusiasm, while the efforts of Freemasonry to de-christianize souls made her passionately indignant.

Her greatest desire and hope would have been to be the mother of a priest, especially a missionary priest. On that account, her joy was exultant when Marie-Joseph-Louis came into the world on September 20, 1866! She wrote: "I believe my fortune is complete"; to Father she pointed out: "Look, how lovely his little hands are! What a glorious day when he'll ascend the altar, or preach from a pulpit!" She already dreamed, in her maternal pride, of the lace alb in Point d'Alençon that she would embroider for him.

The child died; Mamma thought to obtain through his intercession, the cure of his sister, Hélène, who was then suffering from an inflammation of the interior of the ears, which seemed incurable. The prayer was heard, as the mother related to her sister-in-law, five years after the event:

> One day, returning with Hélène from the doctor, who gave me little hope of a cure, and seeing the uselessness of earthly means, I felt an inspiration to have recourse to my little Joseph, who had then been dead five weeks. I told Hélène about little Joseph in Heaven, and directed her to say a prayer to him, asking for her cure. The following morning, the ear was perfectly cured, the "running" had suddenly stopped, and she felt no soreness afterwards. I also obtained several other graces, but less striking than that one.[67]

After the death of her first baby boy, mother made a novena to St. Joseph to obtain another baby aspirant for the priesthood. Nine months afterwards exactly, her prayers were heard, but again she had to make the sacrifice soon after, of seeing him depart for Heaven.

In her personal notes, Marie related:

> When mother accompanied Pauline and me to the Visitation School at Mans, as the train was pass-

---

67. Letter of October 17, 1871.

ing the cemetery she used to rise and look out towards the grave of her little angels. When no stranger was in the carriage, she would prayerfully speak to them out loud.

There was another favor, obtained from Heaven, which is not less striking than that of Hélène's cure, although of a different nature; Mother did not live to see the final effects. In 1873, she wrote to her two older girls:

> I trust that you will both go to Holy Communion on the 8th of December, the Feast of the Immaculate Conception. Don't forget to pray for Léonie.[68]

We know how the life of this child finally ended and how the bitter struggles eventually were crowned by a magnificent victory.

In spite of the great disappointments of her own life, which she offered to God with heroic conformity to His Divine Will, Mother desired at least to offer her children to God in the religious life. When reading the biography of Madame Acarie, whose three daughters had become Carmelite nuns, she exclaimed: "All her daughters Carmelites! Can a mother have so much honor?"

But she was on her guard not to say a word that might exert any indiscreet pressure in regard to their vocations. At home, however, she aimed at an atmosphere of piety, as well as of reverence for everything

---

68. Letter of November 30, 1873.

connected with God. Souls were spontaneously directed towards Him.

She spoke more freely and intimately with Pauline, in a tone of confidence, as with a big sister. The latter was impressed by her explanation of the *white* crown reserved for *virgins who alone will follow the Lamb whithersoever He goeth, and who sing as it were a new canticle which the others cannot sing.*[69]

At one time, Mother thought she saw indications of a religious vocation in Marie, and wrote about it to Pauline:

> Do not tell her this; she would think that I desire it. Truly I desire it only if it be the Will of God for her. Provided that she follow the vocation that He will give her, I shall be happy.[70]

A letter to her sister-in-law helps us to penetrate to the depths of her heart's feelings:

> In spite of my ardent desire to give both of my older girls to God, if He asked me to make the double sacrifice, immediately, I should do so with all my heart, but it would not be without suffering.[71]

Charity towards the Neighbor

In everyone's estimation, as I have already said, Mother was completely unselfish and utterly forgetful

---

69. *Apoc.* 14:3-4.
70. Letter of December 5, 1875.
71. Letter of July 9, 1876.

of self. As a result, she could think of others and devote
herself entirely to their service.

Daughter of a military officer, courage came instinc-
tively to her, and cowardice disgusted her. Duty was the
first of all obligations, duty, not simply towards God, but
towards one's neighbor and towards one's country. In
the war of 1870, at the time of the military mobiliza-
tion, she heard of a lady in the town who had suc-
ceeded in hiding her husband. "Is it possible to do such
a thing?" she exclaimed indignantly.

But if egotism made her indignant, she had but a
smile of pity for the inevitable class distinctions. Pauline
received from her keen pen an example of her clear
judgment. It was in regard to a gala performance at the
Catholic Club that she wrote:

> Two hundred letters of invitation were sent out
> to the "upper class" ladies, and card invitations to
> those of lesser rank; in the hall, also, a dividing bar-
> rier was placed between the two categories.
>
> One of the ladies, who had received only a card,
> yet whose son was one of the principal actors, said
> in protest: "If I am not allowed to go in with those
> who received letters, I shall take my boy away, and
> he will not play at all."
>
> Nevertheless, she was not allowed to pass, and she
> did not dare withdraw her son; but there was gen-
> eral discontent on the part of those having cards.
>
> To prevent a social insurrection, another small
> entertainment was given today, at which no distinc-
> tions were made. The gentlemen who organize these

affairs really do not know what to do to please everybody. It is certain that the great ladies would not
come if they did not have front seats, and on the
other hand, the mothers whose children entertain the
party, are annoyed if they are put in the back seats.

But it is impossible to please everybody. Only in
Heaven will the poor receive the *first seats*. No use
expecting that here below.[72]

She was naturally compassionate, particularly for
those who suffer. Public afflictions deeply moved her
heart and excited her generosity. Thus, in July 1875, she
sent her offering for the flooded areas of Lisieux.

She preferred to exercise charity in the most direct,
immediate way; that is, to give daily help to those who
seemed to be in need around her, and her faith made
her think first of all of souls. Hence she urged us to pray
for sinners, for those in the neighborhood who were in
danger of death. These she visited, and helped materi-
ally, if they needed it; she would tactfully direct their
thoughts to God, and call in the priest when there was
need of the last Sacraments. Her letters contain many
instances of this spiritual form of charity.

In one of her letters, after having recommended to
Pauline's prayers a poor man who was dying after forty
years' neglect of religious practices, she concluded her
letter:

Your father is doing all he can to help him to
decide to receive the last Sacraments, but the dying

---

72. Letter of April 29, 1877.

man imagines he has nothing to do, but, like St. Paul, to receive his crown of justice!

It is true that he is a good man, but he is more difficult to convert than a bad man. Only a miracle of grace can remove the thick scales, which prevent him from seeing things rightly.[73]

A letter from her brother had told of the spiritual return to God of one of his friends. She writes:

I was so interested in his salvation, I prayed all I could, and made a very earnest novena for him, placing all my hope in St. Joseph for his conversion. On that account, I am so happy that he died as a good Christian.[74]

Again, in a letter to Pauline, she refers to one of her lace-workers, who had died suddenly:

I cannot put her out of my mind; but the most painful thing for me is the thought that she did not practice her religion; she went to Mass only two or three times a year.[75]

In another letter to Pauline, she criticizes the timidity of Louise, the housemaid:

The maid has spent a week at home. Her father is dangerously ill, and he will not hear of Confession. I had strongly urged her to notify the priest, in order that he might pay a visit and gradually prepare

73. Letter of May 14, 1876.
74. Letter to her brother, March 19, 1874.
75. Letter of February 26, 1876.

him; but she did not want to do so. She is like her
mother, who repeats: "There is plenty of time: he is
not so ill as that!" That infuriates me to the utmost,
and makes me very annoyed with her.[76]

From her ardent soul, consumed with zeal for the salvation of sinners, rises this sorrowful exclamation:

> O Lord, how sad is a home without religion!
> What a frightful spectre does death appear there![77]

To lead souls back to God, she relied first and above
all else on the efficacy of God's grace obtained by
prayer; but at the same time one can see she did not
ignore the tactful intervention of creatures. Her personal method was a radiating goodness, which was
manifested first to the members of her household.

In his old age, she took her father into her own
home. He was hard to please, but she took care of him
with tireless devotedness, doing everything in her
power to comfort him in his last days. She wished even
to go to Purgatory in his place, and had made the *Heroic
Act*[78] for his sake.

Mother also manifested unlimited solicitude for her
brother, Isidore Guérin. At first, while he was a student
in Paris, she watched over him from afar. As I have
already said, she advised him and sometimes scolded
him, but always with such tactfulness, that he was not
offended. Afterwards, when he was married, her interest

---

76. April 29, 1877.
77. Letter to Pauline November 7, 1875.
78. Letters to her brother, October and November 1868.

in him extended to all the members of his family. She
shared with keen concern in their sorrows, as also in
their joys, while endeavoring to lift up their hearts
through submission and gratitude to divine Providence.

When M. Guérin lost his third child, baby Paul, at
birth, she wrote to him:

> In spite of all, let us not give way to murmuring;
> the good Lord is Master. For our own good He may
> allow us to suffer more and more, but never will His
> help and His grace be lacking to us.[79]

Several years before that, at the time of M. Guérin's
purchase of his chemist shop at Lisieux, she expressed
her regret that it was so far away from Alençon, but the
same heroic confidence is conveyed in these lines:

> I have left all to God's Will and His grace.[80]

When, instead of encouragement and sympathy, her
brother needed a congratulatory or joyful note at the
time of some success, she rejoiced with him. The very
year of her death, when her family was a prey to the most
painful anxiety, she sends this spontaneous outburst:

> Your good news has filled us all with joy, even my
> husband, who is so grieved at the state of my
> health.[81]

The kindness and thoughtfulness of her heart was
also shown to strangers.

---

79. Letter to her brother, October 17, 1871.

80. Letter of April 22, 1866.

81. Letter to her sister-in-law, January 5, 1877.

During the war of 1870, when my mother was obliged to put up nine German soldiers in her home, she noticed one who seemed to be sad and homesick for his family. She did not hesitate to speak to him, and secretly gave him some dainties, for which he showed extreme gratitude.

When she could not go herself, Mamma frequently sent Louise, the maid, to render assistance to needy families. In after years, Louise testified to these acts of charity:

> I alone know how many two franc pieces (of money) as well as the many dishes of stew she sent through me to poor persons around Alençon.[82]

But it was especially her own children whom she taught to be charitable to the suffering poor, and to show them respect. I frequently saw them coming to the house and receiving food and clothing. Mother often shed tears when she heard their tales of distress.

For Léonie's First Communion, Mother selected a poor girl in her class, had her dressed in white also for her First Communion, and invited her to the place of honor at the festive dinner for the occasion.

One day while traveling, she reproved another lady in the railway carriage who showed displeasure at the arrival of a poor woman with her two babies. When they reached Alençon mother helped the woman with her children and parcels to get to her home. Father,

---

82. Letter of Mme. Le Gendre, July 22, 1923.

who had been waiting at the station, also helped; and it was midnight before they reached their own home.

Another instance of their charity has always remained vividly in my mind. I was then seven years old and I recall it as if it were yesterday. My own description of it would be much less interesting than to follow it through mother's pen, when she was writing about it to Pauline:

> We took a long walk in the fields . . . When coming back we met a poor old man, who had a very kind face. I sent Thérèse to give him a little alms. He seemed to be so touched by it, and thanked us so much for it that I understood he must be really needy. I told him to follow us home, and that I would give him some shoes. He came, and we gave him a good dinner; he seemed to be dying of hunger.
>
> I could not tell you how much he has to suffer in his old age. This last winter he had his feet frozen. He sleeps in an abandoned hut, and has nothing whatsoever to live on. He stays close beside the entrance of the military barracks in order to get the remnants of their meals.
>
> Before he left, I told him to come whenever he wished, that I would give him bread. I wish your father could get him into the Hospice for the aged—he himself would like so much to go there. We shall try to arrange that for him.
>
> His wretchedness has made me quite sad. I cannot help thinking about the poor man, who seemed so pleased with the few pieces of money I gave him.

"With these," he said, "I can get some soup; tomorrow I'll go to the 'cheap kitchens.' Then I'll get some tobacco, and have a shave." In a word, he was as happy as a child. While he was eating, he would take up the shoes, turn them over with delight, and smile at them.[83]

Eventually, father had him admitted to the Home for Incurables. The poor old man wept for joy.

I must also mention my mother's intervention on behalf of a poor girl who was being exploited by two hypocritical shrews. The whole affair had to be taken to court. She followed up the case, in spite of many inconveniences and a great deal of trouble, even admitting sadly:

> If we did not work for Our Lord's sake, it would be very discouraging to try to do good.[84]

* * *

To her generous heart the forgiving of injuries and wrongs was as spontaneous as the need she felt of making persons around her happy. A disagreeable neighbor had taken law proceedings against my parents, on account of the collapse of the intervening boundary wall.

Mother relates a part of the incident to Pauline, in these lines:

---

83. Letter of May 14, 1876.
84. Letter of November 1875.

Your father was summoned to court. He explained his case so effectively that all, including the judge, were indignant at the proceedings of our neighbor.

That is the situation at the moment; I do not know how it will end. I am not concerning myself about it very much. We can but accept contradictions patiently, since we must suffer in this world. If only it enables us to avoid a little of Purgatory, we shall bless M.M. in the next world, for having made us undergo some of it in this life. But I prefer that it should be he who should do us this wrong, rather than that we should have to reproach ourselves with having caused him a quarter of the trouble.[85]

On another occasion, it was in regard to a dressmaker whom we had to give up. Her work had been careless, and to make matters worse, not only would she not stand any criticism, but she would not accept any suggestion or advice. Mother wrote to Pauline:

The dressmaker met me Wednesday. I had just bought the material for the children's dresses. The poor woman shed tears in begging my pardon. She clasped my hands with such affection that I felt myself overcome—much less than that suffices to disarm me entirely. So we became completely reconciled.[86]

I have already spoken of how good mother was to the servants of the house, including workmen temporarily

---

85. Letter of March 26, 1876.
86. Letter of March 12, 1876.

employed, gardeners, roofers or masons. Her first concern was to do them some spiritual good, helping them to accept and understand religious truths, and better appreciate the love of God.

When the maid was ill, she took care of her as if she had been her own daughter. Once, it happened that she spent three weeks, day and night, at the bedside of Louise, who had a very severe attack of articular rheumatism, and whom she did not wish to send to the hospital.

Like my father, she always cultivated kindly charity of judgment, and never criticized others in their absence. On that point of charity in word she was almost scrupulous, and sometimes she accused herself with much humility of the witty remarks that came so spontaneously to her, but which might wound charity. At her death it was seen that she had only friends. Many indeed were those who wept for her as their benefactress.

In a letter to her sister-in-law, some weeks before her death, she herself bears witness to the affection in which she was held. She writes about one of her lace-makers, near Alençon.

> As soon as she heard that I was ill, without knowing what was the matter, she came expressly to see me, about two months ago. When I told her the whole situation, she burst into tears, and showed me as much sympathy as if she were my own sister.[87]

---

87. Letter of July 8, 1877.

Abandonment to God, Patience in Trials

From passages in my mother's letters, which I have already quoted, one can see that what characterized her above all was the certainty that God governs all things, that He has a particular love for us, and that whatever He does, is well done. She comes back unceasingly to these truths.

The whole system of education which she gave us was based on this conviction: that we are loved by God, a conviction so deeply impressed in her soul that she lived by it. Referring to her illness, she wrote to her sister-in-law:

> My brother has an idea that God would cure me only if it were for His glory. Personally, I say that everything serves God's glory, but He does not think absolutely of His own glory alone. He would perform a miracle for me, even if no one in the world should know of it but myself.[88]

These sentiments had been always in her soul. In a letter of January 1, 1863, we find this outburst of gratitude and hopefulness:

> When I think of what the good God, in whom I placed all my confidence, and to whom I trusted the care of my business, has done for me and my husband, I cannot doubt but that His divine Providence watches over His children in a particular way.[89]

---

88. Letter of June 7, 1877.
89. Letter to her brother.

It was this assurance of invincible, even audacious, confidence, towards our Father in Heaven, that sustained her in her many trials.

And indeed she well knew anguish in the illnesses of her children, and in the death of four of them. She accepted everything with admirable resignation, notwithstanding a very keen sensitivity, which caused her to suffer greatly from anxieties and separations.

Anxieties! She had many of them. After the death of her two little Josephs, she wrote, referring to a new birth which she was expecting:

> You would not believe how afraid I am, when I think of the little baby that I am awaiting. I imagine that it will be the same as with the other two, and it becomes like a constant nightmare for me. I believe that the fear of it will be worse than the reality. When misfortunes happen, I resign myself to them all right, but the apprehension is a real torture. During Mass, this morning, I had such depressing thoughts that I was all upset by them.
>
> The best thing is to abandon oneself into the hands of the good God, and to wait calmly for events, with full acceptance of His Will. That is what I shall endeavor to do.[90]

And after the birth of the fifth girl, she wrote:

> I was still hoping that it would be a little boy, but if the Lord does not wish it, I am quite resigned to His Will.[91]

---

90. Letter to her sister-in-law, February 29, 1869.
91. Letter to her husband on a business trip, 1869.

This refrain of complete surrender is constantly repeated, both orally and in her letters, no matter what trials she experienced.

* * *

I believe the best way of showing what her dispositions were, at the death of her children is to quote some letters of her Visitation sister. The written expressions, vibrant with emotion, reveal to us also certain significant details in regard to the sentiments of my mother, when she used to beg God for a child, and while she bore the infant in her womb.

At the death of the first little Joseph, who took flight to Heaven after less than five months, Sister Marie Dosithée wrote, February 15, 1867:

> Dearest Sister,
>
> When I received your telegram yesterday evening at 5:30, our little angel was already in Heaven! How can I console you, dear sister? I need consolation myself; my hand is still trembling, and yet I am quite resigned to the will of God. He gave him to us. He has taken him away from us. May His holy Name be blessed!
>
> I must admit to you, that ever since he was born, I had a constant presentiment of what has just happened. *You had begged God for him with such conditions* that in the present state of the world, one could only realize them by dying at the age at which he died!

Yesterday morning, at Holy Communion, I was begging Our Lord to leave him with us, as we wished him to be trained only for His own glory, and for the salvation of poor souls. I thought I heard an interior voice replying to me: *that God wished the first-fruits, and that later on He would give you another child who would realize exactly what we desire.*

She concludes her letter with this affectionate remembrance for her brother-in-law:

And your poor husband, how grieved he must be! Tell him that this letter, and all the sentiments expressed in it, are for him also.

The following year, when the second little Joseph died, at the age of eight months, the Visitation nun again endeavored to console my mother:

How your heart must be broken by this new blow! Oh! yes, the plans of God are impenetrable! I thought He would leave you this child; but He knows better than we, what we need, so let us leave Him free! This life is full of trouble. Dearest, you know something about this by experience; from your childhood up to the present, what troubles of all kinds have you not endured? But happiness will come, too, and the measure of your joy will be proportionate to your sorrows.

Have no doubt about it: "You are now sowing in tears, but you will reap in abundance the joys of the Lord." At the end of this miserable life, you will see your two beautiful little angels coming to meet you, and telling of the mercies of the Lord towards you.

For is it not He who has withdrawn them, from the mud and the corruption of this world, before they could have been soiled by it?

Dear sister, I should love so much to give you some words of consolation, but although I know what the Lord has done is for the best, still I feel a sort of anguish at the departure of the dear little one. And besides, your grief and that of your husband weighs heavily on my heart. I should like to take it wholly on myself and leave none of it to you. But that is impossible; each one must bear her own share. However, I hope Isidore will go to comfort you.

I should advise you, my poor sister, never again to ask God for children. If He sends you others, you will accept them, and if He takes them away, you will allow Him to do so. Endeavor only to educate your girls so well that they will give as much glory to God as the greatest saints. Think, for example: hasn't our Blessed Margaret Mary saved more souls than many missionaries? God makes use of what is weakest to fulfill His designs.

After all, perhaps the Lord, pleased with your resignation, will grant you what you desire. Meanwhile, try not to place any obstacle to grace in your soul, but be faithful to all that God asks of you.[92]

Concerning the death of this second little Joseph, I often heard it said that my mother placed a crown of white roses on his head, and she kept close to his tiny coffin up to the last moment. "My God," she would

---

92. Letter of August 25, 1868.

sigh from time to time, "how hard it is to put him into
the grave, but since You will it so, may Your holy will
be done."

* * *

Two months later, it is over the remains of her dear
old father that she again weeps. Sister Marie Dosithée
writes to M. Guérin, telling him how anxious she is
about the health of their sister, while expressing a beautiful eulogy of her at the same time.

> Poor Zélie is not easily consoled for the many
> losses she has undergone this last year.
> She goes back in memory over the happy
> evenings she had formerly with all her children;
> while the good grandfather, seated beside the fire,
> joined in with the fun of the little ones. Now, they
> are all passed away, the dear old father and the babies
> . . . I am afraid that eventually the health of the
> mother will not withstand so many shocks.
> *However, what gives me some confidence is her spirit of
> faith, and her truly prodigious courage. What a valiant
> woman! She is not dejected by adversity, nor elated by
> prosperity. She is admirable!*[93]

At the death of little Hélène, who was five years old,
the grief of the mother, as well as of the father, was
poignant. Together, they offered her to God. My mother
thought that she would die of grief. She wished, never-

---

93. Letter of Sr. M. Dosithée, October 25, 1868.

theless, in each case, to lay out the deceased child and place it in the coffin herself.

On this occasion, the words of the holy Visitation nun take on a prophetic tone, while acknowledging the excellent dispositions of her sister:

> Sursum corda! Raise up your heart! Our angel is in Heaven, and without having experienced the troubles of this world. She has gone from the arms of her mother into those of Our Lord, clothed in her white baptismal robe. We should have wished to keep her with us; she was so promising, but who can foretell the future? Is she not in possession of true blessedness which she might have lost later on? God is not less lovable when He takes away than when He gives to us.
>
> O my dearest sister, how happy I am to see your deep faith and your resignation! Soon you will possess again those whom you loved so much; and then it will be never to be separated from them. Yes, you will have a beautiful crown!
>
> At present your heart is being crushed, but by its submission to all the divine desires, it sends forth a sweet perfume that rejoices the heart of God.
>
> I cannot help thinking that you are happy to give chosen souls to Heaven, who will be your crown and your joy. And besides, your faith and your unshakable confidence will one day have their magnificent reward.
>
> *Be certain, then, that the Lord will bless you, and that the measure of your troubles will also be that of the consolations stored up for you. In a word, will you not be fully*

rewarded, if the good God, so pleased with you, will grant
you that Great Saint whom you have so much desired for
His glory?[94]

By these words of encouragement, it can be seen that
mother was not unlike her religious sister in sentiments
of invincible faith and blind hope in God. When Mme.
Guérin lost her baby boy at his birth, mother relates her
own edifying feelings in similar circumstances. Here are
a few paragraphs from her letter:

> I am deeply saddened by the sorrow which has
> just come to you; it is indeed a real trial for you. This
> is one of your first troubles, my poor dear sister!
> May Our Lord grant you resignation to His holy
> Will! Your dear little child is with God; he is look-
> ing down on you and loving you; and one day, you
> will possess him again. This is a great consolation
> that I have experienced myself, and which I still
> feel.
>
> When I had to close the eyes of my dear children
> and bury them, I felt deep sorrow, but I was always
> resigned to it. I did not regret the pains and the sor-
> rows which I had endured for them. Many persons
> said to me: "It would have been better for you if you
> had never had them." I could not bear that kind of
> talk. I do not think that the sorrows and the troubles
> endured could possibly be compared with the eternal
> happiness of my children with God. Besides, they are
> not lost to me forever; life is short and filled with
> crosses, and we shall find them again in Heaven.

94. Letter of February 23, 1870.

It was especially the first time that I lost one of my children that I so keenly felt the happiness of having a child with God. The good Lord proved to me in a sensible way that He accepted my sacrifice. I obtained, by the intercession of that little angel, a very extraordinary grace.[95]

In a later letter to her sister-in-law, she repeats the same thoughts:

These two feelings of sorrow and joy are often equally blended in me. We know that life is short, and that soon we shall see them again.[96]

These supernatural views appear again in these lines:

Four of my children are already safe, and the others, yes, the others, too, will reach Heaven, laden with more merits because they will have combatted longer.[97]

Mother herself tells of the remark made by someone who said: "God took away four of her children to relieve her a little of her endless toil." But she strongly protested against that explanation:

That is not the way I look at it. The good Lord is Master of all and does not have to ask permission of me. On the other hand, so far I have borne the burdens of maternity very well, trusting in Divine Providence. Besides, what can be expected? We are

---

95. Letter May 5, 1871 (the cure of little Hélène's ear).

96. Letter of November 5, 1871.

97. Letter to Pauline, March 4, 1877.

not on earth to have great pleasures: those who look for enjoyment are very wrong, and are frightfully disappointed in their expectations.[98]

She frequently repeats the same thought: "We must carry our cross one way or the other."

> We say to Our Lord: "I do not want this, or that." Often our prayer is heard, but often, also, to our own misfortune. It is much better to bear patiently whatever comes our way; joys are always mingled with sorrows.[99]

And again:

> The good Lord does not do things by halves; He always gives what we need. Let us then carry on bravely.

And this God who is so good, she calls, moreover, "*Our Heavenly Father.*"[100]

What mother felt and complained of was that she could not, herself, nurse any but her first three children. She had to give the others out to be nursed, often at a distance in the country, necessitating very fatiguing journeys for her to visit the children.

When Thérèse was born, mother felt an inexpressible joy. Before her birth, she admitted having heard her singing with herself. But soon after her birth, the baby fell ill, and once so seriously that she refused even to

---

98. Letter to Mme. Guérin, May 5, 1871.

99. Letter to Mme. Guérin, October 1, 1871.

100. Letters to her sister-in-law, May 7, 1876 and October 1876.

take the mother's breast. Mamma watched over her night and day, endeavoring to feed her by other means which the doctor ordered.

At one time they thought that she was dead. Another nurse was hurriedly called in, who only shook her head on seeing the condition of the sick baby.

It was then that mother went up to her room, and beseeched St. Joseph to bring the child back to life; at the same time resigning herself to the Divine Will, if God wished to take her to Himself. Trembling with mortal anguish, she went downstairs, to find that the dearest child was saved. One may well believe that the Church is indebted for St. Thérèse of the Child Jesus to the tears and prayers of her mother.

Nevertheless, this semi-resurrection had to be made sure of by a great sacrifice: to let the new nurse take Thérèse off to the country. Mamma wrote:

> What consoles me is that it is the will of God, since I have done all that I could to raise the child myself. [101]

Three weeks afterwards the baby had a new crisis. Mother, accompanied by the doctor, set out immediately for Semallé, where the nurse lived. In a letter to her sister-in-law she described the journey:

> We passed a beautiful castle and magnificent estates. I said to myself: "All that means nothing; we shall be happy only when we and our children shall

---

101. Letter to her sister-in-law, 1873.

all be united in Heaven." When thinking of Thérèse,
I made the sacrifice of her earthly life to God.

And she concludes:

> I have done all in my power to save the life of
> Thérèse. Now, if the good Lord wishes to dispose of
> things differently, I shall try to bear the trial as
> patiently as I can. [102]

Happily, the child recovered completely.

Soon after the illness of Thérèse, Mother was to
manifest again her same *spirit of abandonment,* at the time
of Marie's attack of typhoid fever, which caused
Mother great fatigue. She had undergone much strain
and trouble also during and after the invasion of 1870,
when the family, with all the inhabitants of Rue Pont-
Neuf, were threatened with ruin.

That filial dependence on God radiated from her in
other circumstances where so many parents would find
occasion for disappointment. We find this well summed
up in a letter to her sister-in-law, when each of them
was expecting a child:

> I am delighted at the thought that next August
> we shall each have a baby boy—at least, I hope so.
> But little boy or girl, we must gratefully accept what
> God sends us, for He knows better than we what we
> need most. [103]

After the birth of Marie Guérin and of Melanie

102. Letter to Mme. Guérin, March 30, 1873.
103. Letter of February 12, 1870.

Thérèse Martin, who, alas, was to live but a few weeks, mother returned to the same thought. From her viewpoint, which considered only the immortal soul of her child, it did not matter whether it was a girl or a boy. She wrote to Mme. Guérin:

> If you were like me, you would not mind, for I never feel a moment's disappointment one way or the other.[104]

Whatever happened, we find always the same Christian attitude towards trials; hence, she writes in a philosophical strain to the same correspondent:

> Everyone in the world has troubles; the happiest are only the least unfortunate. The simplest and the wisest thing in all cases is to submit to God's will, and to prepare in advance to bear one's cross as bravely as possible.[105]

She could give this advice, for she followed it herself so perfectly in practice. It was this attitude that enabled her to accept her last illness with the most heroic self-abandonment.

---

104. Letter of August 23, 1870.
105. Letter of February 12, 1870.

MY MOTHER'S ILLNESS AND DEATH

"Because he hoped in me, I will deliver him;
I will protect him because he has known my
name. He shall call upon me, and I will answer
him; I will be with him in trouble. I will rescue
him and I will glorify him." (*Ps.* 4: 14-15).

The Development of Her Illness, and Her Admirable Resignation

As we have seen, Mother was of a rather delicate constitution, and although slight of figure, her extraordinary energy made up for it and enabled her to dominate fatigue.

In the year 1865 she noticed a swelling in her breast. This was the result of an accident years before, in her youth, when she struck herself against the corner of a table. It was a source of great anxiety to Father. Our uncle, M. Guérin, was consulted. No immediate treatment was prescribed. For eleven years nothing serious was feared, but then pain developed, revealing the presence of a cancerous tumor. This spread and after causing her terrible suffering, finally, led to her death.

When the doctor tactlessly announced to her that the illness was incurable, she bore the shock with her habitual spirit of faith. She simply added:

> The only good he did me was the day he told me
> the whole truth; that consultation was, for me,
> beyond all price.

Her unselfish affection manifested itself in consoling all of us, particularly our sorrowing father. With that object in view, and overcoming her own suffering, she valiantly continued her ordinary life of work, abandoning herself to God's will; while uniting with us in our prayers for her recovery. All her correspondence of that time breathed the most complete resignation. She was an object of admiration for the whole family, as well as for the priest who came to encourage her.

Her former maid, Louise Marais—Madame Le Gendre—writing to Carmel, 46 years later, relates the incident:

> During her illness, one day she received at her
> office a call from the parish priest of Montsort, who
> was her confessor, while I was present. She spoke to
> him of her death with so much resignation that the
> priest said: "Madame, I have met many valiant
> women, but never one like you." The good pastor
> was less calm than Madame.

This letter, filled with praise, concludes:

> I could go on endlessly telling you about all her
> acts of kindness, and her resignation to the will of
> the good God.

Indeed her supernatural submission was so deep that she used to say with serenity: "I am afraid of nothing;

our Lord upholds me. The grace of each moment is sufficient, and I shall have that to the very end."

For further proof, here are some extracts from her
letters:

> As for worrying much over my troublesome
> gland, I have not started yet. If the good Lord wishes
> me to die as a result of that, I shall try, as well as
> I can, to be resigned, and to bear my illness
> patiently.[106]

And with what complete detachment she followed
the progress of the disease:

> It is becoming red and inflamed now. To be frank
> with you, I feel a little anxious sometimes, but I do
> not mention it here at home. If it is dangerous, they
> will know it soon enough.
>
> I wish that you would not worry too much about
> me, and that you be resigned to the will of God. If
> He found me very useful here on earth He would
> certainly not permit me to have this illness, for I have
> prayed so hard not to be taken out of this world as
> long as I should be necessary to my children.[107]

In this letter she speaks of the desolation of the
household over the doctor's verdict. Father was "completely crushed and did not even want to leave the
house any more."

---

106. Letter to her sister-in-law, August 20, 1876.
107. Letter to Mme. Guérin, December 17, 1876.

Pilgrimage to the Grotto of Massabielle (Lourdes)

Seeing that the disease was becoming worse, she wrote to her relatives at Lisieux:

> I am looking forward eagerly to a pilgrimage to Lourdes, and if I am necessary for my family, surely I shall be cured, for it is not faith that is lacking in me.

Then she humbly adds:

> I do not merit to have persons so much concerned about me; my life is not so precious. There are so many who believe themselves to be useful, and whom God decides to call away, because, after their death, things will go on even better.[108]

Some weeks later:

> If the good God wills to cure me, I shall be very happy, for in the depths of my heart I desire to live; it is a sacrifice to leave my husband and my children. But, on the other hand, I repeat: "If I am not cured, it will be because it is better for them that I die." [109]

Friends recommended her to the prayers of several religious communities at Lourdes. All her hope lay in the pilgrimage.

> Really, I depend now only on the help of our Blessed Mother. I am not, however, convinced that

108. Letter to Mme. Guérin, January 28, 1877.
109. Letter of February 20, 1877.

she will cure me, for it is quite possible that such is not the will of God. Then, we must be resigned, and I assure you that I am.

Oh, how I wish there would be no more talk about all this! What good does it do? Everything possible has been done; let us leave the rest in the hands of Providence. If I am not cured, it means that God is "holding firm" and He wants me.[110]

She herself was "holding firm" to obtain the object of her prayers. She wrote to her sister-in-law:

I shall return to Lourdes in six months if I obtain nothing this time. The worse I feel, the more I shall have.[111]

In order that the pilgrimage might be completely supernatural in its object, she set aside all thought of an excursion.

In that way I shall have more confidence. I prefer also to go without Louis. Through kindness he would want to take me from city to city, in order to make the journey pleasanter, and I should not be cured.[112]

She wanted to travel with her three older girls, while admitting at the same time:

---

110. Letter of January 5, 1877.
111. Letter of March 12, 1877.
112. Letter of March 12, 1877.

It is a lot of trouble and expense; but it seems to me the more sacrifices we make, the more the Blessed Virgin will be disposed to listen to us.[113]

She wrote to Pauline:

At first your father did not approve of my taking the three of you, but now he wants it himself. He says that we cannot make too many sacrifices to obtain such a great miracle.

Pauline was so convinced the miracle would be granted that to avoid all disillusionment Mother wrote her these lines:

We must prepare ourselves to be ready to accept generously the will of God, whatever it may be. It will always be what is best for us.[114]

Two months previously, she had encouraged her in the same way:

Let us surrender ourselves to His goodness and His mercy; He will settle everything for the best.[115]

In February, 1877, she had expressed the same feelings to Mme. Guérin:

I am relying on the pilgrimage to Lourdes. But if I am not cured, I shall try to sing the hymns just the same on our return journey.

---

113. Letter to her sister-in-law, May 29, 1877.
114. Letter to Pauline, May 1877.
115. March 12, 1877.

Her brother and sister-in-law received the latest report on her health before her departure:

> Last night especially, I suffered very much for two hours. It is no longer possible for me to touch the sore spot; it is too sensitive. I should not be surprised if it broke open before I start. If only no hemorrhage occurs; for that happens, it seems, when a growth opens.[116]

On the Return from Lourdes

> Alas! I am not cured; on the contrary the journey has made my illness worse.

Such was Mother's exclamation on her return from Lourdes. She then related to her Lisieux friends the vicissitudes of her journey:

On her arrival at the Marian shrine, after she had seen about some food for the children, she added:

> As for myself, I took nothing; as I desired first to go to the grotto, then to the piscina for a bath, although I felt completely worn out.

She then gave a vivid account of her mishaps. She missed a step on the stairs of the front porch, and twisted her neck, an incident which will be frequently referred to later. Four times she bathed in the piscina, and each time she almost fainted when she plunged into the cold water. Marie lost her Visitation aunt's

---

116. Letter of June 7, 1877.

rosary beads, the only souvenir of her which mother had. Again, accidentally, she tore her dress so badly that she could not go on until she mended it. Finally we read in her conclusion:

> Nothing but one accident after another, and miseries without number.[117]

At the station of Mans, on their return journey, Pauline left them and went back at once to the Visitation, for the end of the school year. A few days afterwards, June 25th, Mother wrote to her:

> Your father was waiting an hour for us, with the two little ones. Although sad-looking, he was happy to see us again. He had spent painful hours since last Thursday, hoping each moment for the famous telegram, and thrilled with expectation every time the doorbell rang. He was quite surprised to see me returning as cheerfully as if I had obtained the hoped-for miracle. It gave him new courage and the whole house was filled with cheerfulness.

After having recalled the promise of the Blessed Virgin to Bernadette: "I shall not make you happy in this world, but in the next," she concludes:

> In the same way, do not hope for many joys here below, otherwise you would have too many disappointments. For myself, I know by experience what to think of earthly joys. If I did not hope for the joys of Heaven, I should be very unhappy.

---

117. Letter to her brother and sister-in-law, Alençon, June 24, 1877.

> Pray with confidence to the Mother of Mercies;
> she will come to our help with the goodness and
> sweetness of the tenderest of mothers.[118]

Before taking the train for Lourdes, Mother had
stopped at the Visitation Convent of Angers; fervent
prayers were being offered there to obtain the miracle
of her cure. A strange thing happened there at the very
time that she was leaving Lourdes on her return.
Mother relates it herself:

> At 8 o'clock in the evening they heard a small
> cloister bell ringing of itself. The nuns went around
> making inquiries, but nobody had touched the bell.
> They all believed it was the signal for the expected
> miracle, and that it was Our Lady of Lourdes who
> was notifying them that the miracle had taken place
> . . . or rather that it had not taken place![119]

For us, who know the end of the story, was it not a
sign that, in spite of appearances to the contrary, our
Blessed Mother was tenderly watching over the dear
patient and her family?

Sublime Courage Under the Weight of the Cross

In her letter of July 8, 1877, to our aunt at Lisieux,
mother gave details of the still more rapid development
of her illness:

---

118. Letter of June 25, 1877.
119. Letter to her brother and sister-in-law, June 24, 1877.

Not only is the disease continuing to make progress, but the sore has been discharging for the past two weeks. Any effort on my part makes me suffer tremendously, especially since last night.

I had to start at 5 o'clock this morning in order to go to the first Mass; I was alone, as Louis was at Nocturnal Adoration. Finally, I called Marie to help me to dress. In church, I found it very hard to sit down, and to get on my knees. I could scarcely move without crying out; so I am not going back to High Mass again.

Besides that, this last week I have felt a great general weakness which takes all my strength.

In her habitual self-forgetfulness, she leaves the subject of her ailment to the very end of her letter, and then adds in an off-hand manner:

I return to my illness, since you want to have the details. I feel such violent pains in my neck that my husband and Marie believe the Blessed Virgin will surely cure me. They think that she would not permit such an accumulation of mishaps and pains at the same time, since so much of the suffering is the result of my pilgrimage.

Some time afterwards, she again refers to the same distressing subject:

The disease is becoming worse from day to day. I can no longer dress nor undress alone. The arm on the sore side is practically paralyzed, but my hand and fingers can still hold a needle!

Besides, I feel sore, as it were, all over, owing to a constant fever for the past two weeks. I can no longer stand upright, and must remain seated.

I candidly confess that a miracle seems to be very doubtful now. I have definitely come to that conclusion, and I am trying to arrange things as if I were really to die very soon. It is absolutely necessary for me not to lose the little time that I now have to live. These are days of salvation for me that will never return again, and I wish to profit by them.

In that way, I shall have double profit: I shall suffer less by being resigned, and while here on earth I shall put in part of my Purgatory. Ask for me, I beseech you, both resignation and patience, for I need them very much. You know what little patience I have.[120]

Some days later, after having given details of a torturing night, she continued.

Louis, Marie, and the maid stayed beside me the whole time. Poor Louis would take me, from time to time, into his arms, like a child.

I cannot write any more to you. My sight is nearly gone, and my weakness is extreme. A sister-infirmarian is coming today to take care of me.[121]

On the Summit of Calvary

Here I must introduce a number of excerpts from the letters of my sister Marie, written to our aunt at Lisieux.

---

120. Letter of July 15,1877.
121. Letter to her brother and sister-in-law, July 27, 1877.

These health reports will be more eloquent than any comment on my part. By them we shall assist, like the Mother of Sorrows on Calvary, at the last sufferings of our incomparable mother. They give the atmosphere of those sorrow-laden hours.

The first letter is dated July 28, 1877, only a month before the final struggle:

Since the beginning of the week, Mamma has been much worse. On Sunday she still wanted to go to the first Mass; but she needed superhuman courage and had to make incredible efforts to get as far as the church. Every step she took seemed to react on the pains in her neck. Sometimes she was obliged to stop in order to regain a little strength.

When I saw that she was so exhausted, I begged her to return home, but she wanted to go on to the end, believing that the suffering was but a passing attack. It was by no means that; on the contrary she had much trouble on the return journey, so she will not again be so imprudent.

Besides, it would be impossible for her at present, for, since last Monday, she has been unable to leave the house. She no longer goes to her office; Louise and I attend to the lace-workers. Mamma is continually in her room, either lying on the bed, or seated in an armchair. She feels very uncomfortable in bed, on account of her neck, which causes her frightful suffering.

We have put four pillows behind her shoulders, in order that she may be in practically a sitting position in bed; she has to keep her neck absolutely straight, without moving it at all. When she is tired from having her head in that one position, we raise her very gently with the pillows until she is sitting erect. But every change of position means incredible suffering, for the least movement makes her utter piercing cries.

And yet, with what patience and resignation she is bearing this dreadful illness! Her rosary beads never leave her fingers; she is praying constantly in spite of her sufferings. We all have great admiration for her; she has such courage and surpassing energy.

Until two weeks ago she used to recite the five decades of her beads on her knees, before the Blessed Virgin, in my room, which she loves so much. Seeing her so ill, I wanted to have her sit down, but it was useless to ask her.

Mamma quite approves of your idea of coming to Alençon, for we cannot go to Lisieux this year. She would like to have you arrange your trip for the week after the feast of the Assumption, because if the Blessed Virgin were to cure her that day, we should all go to Lisieux, as already planned. Let us hope that the dear Mother will have pity on us, and that she will be touched by our prayers and our tears.

P.S. I forgot to mention that Doctor X came to see mother today. He ordered a sedative for the pains in her neck which, he explained, are the effect of her illness. I thought so myself, for a simple strain would not last so long.

He was very polite and very kindly. I think he does not frighten her so much now.

As to myself, I was only eight years old when my mother, at my request, showed me the sore; I have always kept an unforgettable memory of it. All the upper part of the right side of her breast as far as the shoulder and the base of the neck was bright red with inflammation, while darker red streaks ran through it, up and down.

M. and Mme. Guérin came to Alençon on the 30th of July. After their return to Lisieux, Marie wrote regularly to give news of the dear invalid:

> Since you left, Mamma continues to suffer more and more, and there are new trials every day. For the past two or three days she has constantly complained of heart seizures. She passes very bad nights, and it is absolutely heart-rending to listen to her moaning.
>
> Yesterday evening, she was suffering so much that she kept saying out loud: "Ah! my God, You see that I have no longer any strength left to suffer. Have pity on me! Since I must remain here on this bed of pain, without anyone being able to give me relief, I beg You not to abandon me."
>
> Sometimes she weeps, and keeps looking at us one after the other. Then she says:
>
> "Ah! my poor children. I can no longer take you for a walk, although I have been so anxious to make you happy! And I had so desired to give all the pleasure I could to Pauline during her holidays; now I must leave her to herself, or let her go out without me! O dear little ones, if I could only go with you, how happy we should be."

In a word, our poor dear mother forgets herself to such a point that she is happy only when she sees us going off for a walk. In order to please and humor her, Papa took my sisters for a boat excursion. But what pleasure can we find, when we know our mother is so ill?

Mamma wrote last Sunday to Abbé Martignon of Our Lady of Victories, in Paris, and to the Sisters at Lourdes. We began on Monday the novena that is to close on the feast of the Assumption. I am making it with the greatest confidence. I trust that the Blessed Mother will not abandon us. If she does not cure Mamma she will at least bring her relief, and diminish her suffering, which seems to be growing in intensity.

Whom would the Blessed Virgin protect if she would not protect Mamma, who is so good and so courageous? Last Sunday morning she again wanted to rise in order to go to the first Mass, because she thought that her neck was not so sore, and that she could move it more easily. If you only knew, dear Aunt, all the difficulty I had to keep her from rising. If she could have dressed herself alone, she certainly would have done it.

Last Friday morning she went to the seven o'clock Mass, because it was the First Friday of the month. Papa helped her along, for, without him she could not have gone at all. On arriving at the church, she admitted that if somebody were not with her, she would never have been able to push open the door of the church![122]

---

122. Letter of August 9, 1877.

It was when she was very ill that the following touching incident took place. One day, as Pauline was alone with her beside her bed, Mamma took her hand, and respectfully kissed it. Was this not like a prophecy of the mission which Pauline was to fulfill later on, of being 50 years Prioress of her Carmelite convent, and of three of her own sisters?

Meanwhile, what was becoming of Thérèse and myself in the midst of the confusion and dismay that reigned in the house?

I remember how each morning, a relative used to come for us and let us spend the day in her home. One day we had not had time to say our morning prayers before leaving. Along the way, I whispered to Thérèse: "Should we say that we did not recite our prayers?" "Oh! Yes," she replied. Then, rather bashfully, I confided my secret to the lady, who replied immediately: "Oh! well, my little girls, you can recite them now." Then, leaving us all alone in a big room, she went off. Astonished, I gazed at my sister, who was not less bewildered than I. And she exclaimed: "Ah! That is not like Mamma! She always said the prayers with us!"

If our dear mother was no longer able to teach us to pray, she was resolute in making a great effort in order to take part in our distribution of prizes. Marie, who was our teacher, had organized a little festival to close the school work. Our beloved mother desired, with Papa, to crown the successes of her two little ones. Seated each in a specially draped armchair, they presided together at this last happy family gathering.

Alas! after this last ray of sunset, we had to re-enter the dark tunnel of the bitter preoccupations of the moment.

The hoped-for miracle did not take place on the 15th of August. Our saintly patient bowed, as always to the Divine Will. On the following day, she traced with a trembling hand some lines to her brother; but, her soul strong to the very end, she concludes with this act of self-surrender:

> *What can be done? If the Blessed Virgin does not cure me, that means my time here is at an end, and the good God wishes me to rest elsewhere than upon this earth.*
>
> Z. Martin.

These were the last words that she wrote here below!

Saintly Death

Marie then continued her sorrowful journal to our aunt at Lisieux, on August 25:

> I have sad news to tell you. Mamma is very much worse. Her illness is making frightful progress from day to day. The nights are terrible for her. She is obliged to rise every quarter of an hour, as her suffering prevents her from remaining in bed.
>
> The least little noise brings on terrible crises. Even a whisper, or walking barefoot, wakes her up. Her sleep is so light that the slightest sound awakens her.
>
> For the past two days she appears to be less nervous, and her pains do not seem to be so violent or acute as at the beginning of the week. On Monday

and Tuesday we did not know what to do. Her sufferings were atrocious. We could not relieve her in any way, and no remedy seemed to quiet her.

These incredible tortures have given way to an extreme weakness. She is no longer able to utter a moan—she has not enough strength—and one can scarcely hear her when she speaks. It is only by the movement of her lips we can understand what she wishes to say. Yesterday she was weak, but today she is still weaker.

Last night she had a hemorrhage, which has increased her weakness. Papa spent the whole night beside her; he was so distressed. Fortunately, the hemorrhage did not last long. It seems that it is very dangerous.

I hope that Mamma will regain a little strength and that she will not remain as weak as she is today. It is true that she seems to suffer less, but the weakness frightens me. When she is asleep, one would say that she were no longer living; that is the impression it gives.

Do you believe, Auntie, that this weakness will last long? I think that she would overcome it if she would take some nourishment, but nothing seems to agree with her. Her whole nourishment consists of two or three cups of bouillon, and even that much she cannot always retain.

On the following day, August 26, Marie sent to her uncle this cry of alarm:

Yesterday, I forgot to tell Auntie that Mamma's legs have become swollen, and Papa wishes me to write to you about it immediately. I would have written about it, anyway, for I am very disturbed myself.

The swelling began about a week ago. I realized it only this morning; until then I did not pay much attention to it. Her arm is quite swollen, and she can scarcely move it at all.

Besides that, she is in a state of complete exhaustion. Today, even more than yesterday, she can speak only by signs. If she were left alone in her room, she would die rather than call for help.

She also has just had another hemorrhage. All this has changed her very much, making her emaciated! Papa is so anxious that he has just told me to beg you to come as soon as possible, in order that you may at least find her fully conscious.

It was the evening of August 26th, or the following morning, before the arrival of M. and Mme. Guérin, that she received the Last Sacraments. Thérèse alone mentions it. She writes:

The ceremony of Extreme Unction made a deep impression on me.

It also left a lasting impression on my soul. We were all kneeling beside her bed, in order of age, with Thérèse beside me. Our poor dear father could not restrain his grief.

As for our mother, she remained calm and self-possessed. She was to die thus in a truly saintly way, giving us, to the very end, the example of complete self-forgetfulness and most lively faith.

In the moments of anguish during her malady, her sorrowful plea would rise to Heaven: "Oh! Thou Who hast created me, have mercy on me!" And God had pity on her by hastening the progress of her disease; for, at that time, there were not, as now, sedatives to relieve the pains of poor sufferers.

It was on Tuesday, August 28, 1877, half an hour after midnight, that our admirable mother was taken from us. She was only forty-five years and eight months old.

Supernatural Aftermath

On the morning after her death, our dear father took Thérèse into his arms. "Come," he said, "and kiss your dearest mother for the last time." Without saying a word she pressed her lips to the icy forehead of our dearly beloved mother.

In the course of the afternoon, the young child stood before the coffin left standing in the hallway. She indeed "found it very big and very sad."

In her turn, Marie has left us the expression of her own recollections:

> During the course of the day I often went close to the body of my dear mother. I never tired of looking at her. She seemed to be but 20 years old. I thought that she was beautiful. I felt a supernatural impression as I stood beside her. It struck me, which was quite true, that she was not dead, but more alive than ever.

As for myself, I questioned Pauline, a few days afterwards, about Mamma's death. In particular I asked her if she herself had not received some sign from Heaven of Mother's happiness.

She told me that, in a dream, she had seen an Angel writing on a stretch of sand, shining with light: "*Blessed are those that mourn, for they shall be comforted.*"

How often, in the course of years, our father spoke to us of our "saintly" mother! He always referred to her with that adjective, which was so expressive of his thoughts. Even several years after the event, he wrote in a letter to a friend of his youth:

> In a recent letter I mentioned my five daughters, but I forgot to tell you that I also have four other children, who are with their saintly mother in Heaven, where we hope one day to join them.[123]

My aunt, Mme. Guérin, both pleased and touched by the affection which we showed her, wrote these lines to Sister Thérèse of the Child Jesus, November 16, 1891.

> What have I ever done that God has surrounded me with such affectionate hearts? I only responded willingly to the last pleading look of a mother, whom I loved with all my heart. I feel that I understood that look, which nothing can ever make me forget; it is deeply engraved in my heart. From that moment, I have always endeavored to take the place of her whom God took from you. But alas, no one can replace a mother such as she was! *Ah! my dear*

---

123. Letter to M. Nogrix, 1883.

Thérèse, you had parents that are of those who can be called saints, and who merit to bring forth saints.

Towards the end of her life, our former housemaid, Louise Marais, wrote July 22, 1923.

> In my acute sufferings, I invoke the aid of little Thérèse, and at the same time, of her good and saintly Mamma. If little Thérèse is a saint, I believe that her mother is also a great saint. She had a great many trials during her life, and she accepted them all with resignation. And how eager she was to sacrifice herself constantly!

A friend, Mme. Tifenne, who had always known the family—including our grandfather, the devout Captain Martin—addressed these lines to the Carmelite Convent, after the publication of the *Story of a Soul,* in 1898:

> It was with heartfelt interest that I read all the details given about your family and ancestors. Those whom I knew, together with your father and your saintly mother, made me realize what a line of saints you possess in your family.

About 30 years later, she noted again:

> I pictured your mother to myself again, in the corner of her window with little Thérèse, and I repeated to myself: "Oh, if I had known the gift which God granted to me, when I used to breathe the air of all that holy family, how much better would I have profited by it!"

On the occasion of the centenary of the birth of my mother in 1931, the Reverend Pastor of St. Denys-sur-Sarthon erected in the baptistry of his church, a statue of St. Thérèse, and a commemorative tablet of the Baptism of our mother.

Although deprived, so young, of her mother, Thérèse could proclaim in her favor:

> God, in His goodness, did me the favor of awakening my intelligence when I was still very young ... His design, no doubt, was to make me know and appreciate *the incomparable mother He had given me,* but alas, His divine hand soon took her from me to crown her in Heaven.

I have myself often regretted that I had not been able to appreciate my mother for a longer time, but she was spoken of so often among us that she continued to live, as it were, in our midst. We felt that she was watching over us, and had not left us.

In Carmel, Mother Agnes of Jesus, and Sister Marie of the Sacred Heart recalled her memory with deep feeling. They stressed particularly her invincible *confidence and her abandonment* to divine Providence. They declared that she was never known to fail in these virtues, nor in a *heroic fidelity to the duties of her state of life.*

In a word, always active, always devoted, constantly smiling, our mother never appeared to be doing anything extraordinary, but with remarkable simplicity and humility, she tirelessly spent herself for others, and lived always for the good God.

In listening to these eulogies, and recalling what I had seen myself, I have often said to myself, that our Thérèse inherited those fundamental dispositions which were to make her:

THE APOSTLE OF THE LITTLE WAY.

APPENDICES

SOME TOPOGRAPHICAL DETAILS OF ALENÇON

The Home at Rue St. Blaise, in which St. Thérèse was born, and where our saintly mother died.

Our maternal grandfather, M. Guérin, had bought the house, and had intended to add another story to it, but this was never done. Instead of that, in the garden attached to the house, he had a small annex built, which was connected by an alley. Mother always regretted that the garden, already small, was made still smaller by this additional building.

The ground floor of the home, facing the street, comprised three rooms. The front room, lighted by two windows, was both sitting room and office. It was here that mother worked on her "Point d'Alençon" and received her lace-workers. A large table of oak was in the center of the room (which at that time had a parquet wood floor).

Behind a glass partition was the dining room. But when guests came, or there was a large dinner, the front room was used, the central table being moved against the wall.

Opening into the regular dining room was the

kitchen, which faced a small yard at the back. This serves, at present, as a sacristy and parlor for the Sisters who act as custodians of the place.

On the first floor there are two rooms, facing the (street) balcony. The one on the left—a guest room—has two windows. If necessary, it became a reception room, for the bed was completely hidden in an alcove, closed by a double folding door. In the middle of the room was a round table with a marble top; sideways was a chest of drawers, and a writing desk, all in mahogany. The room was furnished with upholstered chairs and armchairs.

Some of those pieces of furniture have been brought to Lisieux, and are found in Father's room at the Buissonets. The clock and candelabra, now in the dining room at the Buissonets, were formerly on the mantlepiece of the "big room," as it was called.

The other room, facing the balcony, was the bedroom of the older girls, Marie and Pauline. It was there that Marie gave lessons to her young sisters.

Behind the "big room" was that of our parents; an opening has been made from it into the present-day chapel. This room was directly over the kitchen, and was lighted by a window looking out over the small yard. The actual bed and furniture belong to that time. Unfortunately the cradle and crib of Thérèse have disappeared.

On the second floor were the rooms of the children and the maid.

The Garden

To go from the house to the garden, one has to pass by a narrow alley, between the high walls of the adjacent houses; the passage is about 40 feet long. At the end of this alley, on the left, is the sheltered recess where Thérèse and Celine used to count their "sacrifices." That used to mystify their neighbor who from her overlooking window could hear their "debates" about the "sacrifices." Her house was afterwards purchased and is now occupied by the Sisters, who are custodians of the house.

On the right of the passage, at its extremity, is the "annex"—the addition, which grandfather built for the house. It comprised, on the lower floor, a large room, which was used as a laundry and linen room. In the mysterious dream which Thérèse had in her childhood, it was here she saw the two little devils, terrified by the gaze of the child. This incident is referred to in *The Story of a Soul*.

There was another room upstairs. It was there that Thérèse and Celine slept on the night of August 28th, when Mme. Martin breathed her last. Pauline spent the night with them. Immediately after the death of the mother, their uncle Guérin came to notify Pauline, and called to her from the garden: "Your mother is much worse," and added in a low voice: "She is dead." Pauline was so struck and bewildered that she did not wake us.

After the Beatification of St. Thérèse, in order to arrange the property as a place of pilgrimage, the neighboring property was purchased. This allowed for the construction of the chapel, and the placing of a statue of St. Thérèse, which occupies the exact spot of the annex-building, which was torn down.

The garden was quite small, but very gay, with a profusion of flowers, and with fruit trees, trained against the surrounding high wall. The garden measured about 36 feet by 24. A trellised vine surrounded it.

New Constructions

On the right of the house in which St. Thérèse was born a chapel now stands. From the crypt on the ground floor two large staircases, one on each side, lead up to the sanctuary which has an opening into the room where the Saint was born.

On the left of the house, a kind of corridor leads to the statue of the Saint; and towards the site of the annex-building near the garden, there has been built a large room with three façade windows looking to the street.

This was planned in order to house some pieces of furniture, given by Mme. Tifenne, a close friend of the family. Thérèse and I used to spend a part of our holidays with her, in a large room covered with red damask. St. Thérèse used to refer to it as the "Cardinal's room." In the library were preserved the book prizes of Marie and Pauline, formerly in their room, and some paintings from the Buissonets. Other pieces of furniture are preserved as souvenirs, in the room of our parents, where the Saint was born.

Burial Place of my Mother

Mother was first buried in the cemetery of Alençon. Then, in 1894, our uncle Guérin had her remains exhumed to have them placed beside those of my father, in the family vault constructed in the cemetery of Lisieux. Several members of the family were also transferred at that time, at least those who could be identified. The remains of the four little children, who had died in their infancy, were among them.

When he told us about the exhumation of Mother, my uncle said that the coffin was quite intact after 17 years, although another, more recently interred, had entirely disintegrated. He noticed, with emotion, that in the interior nothing had collapsed, and that the folds of the coffin drapery had remained in place, just as when she had been placed in the coffin. But he did not dare to raise them . . .

As the earth in which the coffin had been placed was damp, some small openings were bored at the base of the coffin, and a little water seeped through. That may explain how in the interior nothing had changed in volume.

The granite tombstone was later placed in the garden of the Pavilion at Alençon where it can still be seen.

* * *

At Lisieux no one has been placed in the family vault since 1894. There the monument, striking in its simplicity, with its beautiful circular-armed cross of granite, had the words: "O Crux Ave, spes unica!" (Hail Cross, our only hope!), and "Here rest the parents of the Saint of Lisieux, St. Thérèse of the Child Jesus." (Translator).

IN MEMORIAM

I loved my mother's gentle smile,
Her thoughtful glance that said, the while:
"Eternity doth me, from you, beguile.
I go to Heaven, my God, to be with Thee."

"I go to find, in realms above,
My angel-band in Mary's love.
The children whom I leave below. Ah, prove
Jesus, to them, their guide and stay, always!"

Saint Thérèse of the Child Jesus.
(Translated. Susan Emery).

Prayers to ask for the glorification of the father and mother of St. Thérèse of the Child Jesus, and for graces through their intercession.

O Lord Jesus, who didst make of Thy servant Louis Martin a model husband and father, grant, we beseech Thee, to glorify him who, by his fidelity to Thy laws, his generosity in offering all his children, and his admirable resignation in trials, merited to give the Church St. Thérèse of the Child Jesus.

In Thy goodness, deign to make known Thy designs in his regard, by granting us, through him, the graces for which we ask. Amen.

O God, our Father, who glorified the humble Thérèse for her abandonment and filial confidence in Thee, grant our request that her mother, Zélie Martin, may be proposed by the Church as an example of these same virtues, which she practiced with such a spirit of faith, in the duties and trials of family life.

Grant also, by heavenly favors, to manifest her favorable influence with Thee. Amen.

Persons who receive favors by the intercession of Louis Martin and Zélie Martin are requested to make them known to the Carmel of Lisieux, Calvados, France.

Imprimatur ✝ François-Marie,
Bishop of Bayeux and Lisieux,
February 12, 1954.

The Cause for Louis and Zélie Martin

The processes for the canonization of the Servants of God Louis and Zélie Martin, the parents of St. Thérèse of the Child Jesus, were instigated separately by the dioceses of Bayeux-Lisieux and Sées between 1957 and 1960. The causes were then forwarded to Rome and presented to the Congregation for the Causes of Saints as one single study or *positio*.

On March 26, 1994, Pope St. John Paul II declared Louis and Zélie (Guérin) Martin "Venerable," recognizing their "heroic virtue." On October 19, 2008, the couple was beatified in Lisieux, several months after the Church's official recognition of a healing miracle through their intercession.

On Wednesday, March 18, 2015, Pope Francis authorized the promulgation of the decree recognizing a second healing miracle attributed to the intercession of Blessed Louis and Zélie Martin. Cardinal Angelo Amato, prefect of the Congregation for the Causes of Saints, has announced that they will be canonized in October 2015, to coincide with the world Synod of Bishops on the family. It will be the Church's first joint canonization of a married couple.

CPSIA information can be obtained
at www.ICGtesting.com
Printed in the USA
LVOW10s0100030117
519506LV00001BA/2/P